The VINTAGE TABLE

The VINTAGE TABLE

Personal TREASURES and Standout SETTINGS

Jacqueline deMontravel
and the editors of
Romantic Homes Magazine

PRINCIPAL PHOTOGRAPHY BY
JAIMEE ITAGAKI

CLARKSON POTTER/PUBLISHERS
NEW YORK

Copyright © 2009 by Action Pursuit Group, LLC

Published in the United States by Clarkson Potter/
Publishers, an imprint of the Crown Publishing Group,
a division of Random House, Inc., New York.
www.crownpublishing.com
www.clarksonpotter.com

CLARKSON POTTER is a trademark
and POTTER with colophon is a registered
trademark of Random House, Inc.

Library of Congress Cataloging-in-Publication Data
is available upon request.

ISBN 978-0-307-46054-7

Printed in China

Design by Laura Palese
Additional photographs by Ellen Silverman
and Mark Tanner

10 9 8 7 6 5 4 3 2 1

First Edition

TO ALLAN K. ROSEN,

WHO LET ME INTO HIS HOME
WHEN I WAS A STRANGER. NOW LOOK!

CONTENTS

INTRODUCTION

A beautiful and welcoming vintage table flawlessly combines heirlooms, one-of-a-kind finds, and a few unexpected accents. In such a setting, the time-honored clink of crystal and silver punctuates a room. Surprising results occur when your mother's wedding pieces come together with newer finds. You can draw inspiration from magical places— a midsummer night's dream, Christmas Eve, any flight of the imagination that involves fairies and, of course, a little mischief. The occasion can be a lavish affair or merely an opportunity to test your latest indulgent recipe.

A year of dining with Vintage Vavoom, as we call this style, is a happy one. To dine with an assortment of your favorite pieces is to live life at its most inspiring. Enchantment fills a home when it is called to perform at its most convivial—to entertain family and friends. Recipes beckon from note cards in your grandmother's handwriting, splattered with batter.

⌒ PRECEDING PAGE:
A jam session of great elements placed at different elevations produces an *opulent* effect.

⌒ RIGHT: A *mix and match* of china collected from trips to estate sales, flea markets, and sojourns to France comes together in a dazzling display.

⌒ OPPOSITE, RIGHT: An innovative tabletop need not follow the prescribed accents for china and silver. Use a *chandelier* as a centerpiece, and unite your design elements with shades of white, ornate *silhouettes*, and shimmers from reflective surfaces.

You may even bake with her cookie cutters or ones you've found that have a striking resemblance to hers. Food and style mesh as a feast for the eyes, and become all the more enjoyable when you eat them using beloved possessions. Different times of year bring varied pleasures, from a summer day beneath a wrought-iron trellis to an autumn eve in a weathered barn, with its rough textures complementing the chillier temperatures. Seasonal changes and holidays are causes for celebration and are reflected in the bounty you find in the market, the arrangement of the cupboard, the design on your favorite tablecloth, and, inevitably, in how you realize all of these elements on the table. These annual celebrations are the perfect opportunity to make cherished pieces a part of family traditions.

A table with modern vintage style draws from the best trends of the past arranged with today's sensibility. The designer of these settings may scour the

Internet for the perfect café au lait bowl, ecstatic when she discovers a selection of unexpected colors and finds that they will go perfectly with the more time-tested items she owns. A collection of old and new pieces provides the poetic words to create a sonnet distinguished by function and style.

The vintage table setting does not follow precise rules. Arranging one is not a chess game but rather an easy, playful round of checkers. It is textural and layered. A variety of unlike pieces somehow come together.

To be a hostess with Vintage Vavoom means continually testing new ideas. You might mix and match French hemp linens with remnants found at a flea market or pull together a variety of china through shared colors and textures. Such settings offer a lot to look at—perhaps even twice, as each glance may reveal something new to tickle the senses. A table set with personalized pieces is a table like no other.

∽ GET READY, SET! ∾
USE WHAT YOU'VE LEARNED
TABLETOP DIARY

At the end of each chapter you will be able to gather what you've learned and, in a manner of speaking, put it all on the table. In the same fashion that experienced professionals create sumptuous events for a living, you can utilize one of their trusted tools: an inspiration binder. This collection that you will create can include everything from magazine clippings to company pamphlets, cards, or printouts from websites of florists and bakeries to swatches of fabric and Pantone chips—anything that helps you achieve your goals for the event.

During your reading experience, a particular vignette may spur you to send out those invitations even sooner. A flower arrangement or color palette may be your impetus to start polishing the neglected silver or to arrange a motley combination of dishes and colors. A tabletop diary will help you achieve the best settings imaginable, ones that will show your personal style—for your own enjoyment, and for your guests'.

This diary will help you record your ideas, leaving you with a reference you can keep forever. Inevitably, you will come up with something worth throwing a party for. Isn't that precisely the point?

GETTING STARTED

WHAT YOU'LL NEED:

- One LOOSE-LEAF BINDER, ideally with pockets
- NOTEBOOK PAPER, lined and unlined
- Binder DIVIDERS (make your own or purchase ready made)
- LABELS for dividers
- PENS, PENCILS, CRAYONS, etc.
- SCISSORS
- THREE-HOLE PUNCH
- Top-loading clear-plastic SHEET PROTECTORS
- Other supplies: MAGAZINES from which to cut clippings, copies of favorite PHOTOS, COLOR CHIPS, fabric SWATCHES, etc., for inspiration, information, and collages
- OPTIONAL: fabric, paper, stickers, labels, or other materials to cover or embellish a plain binder

PREPARING YOUR TABLETOP DIARY

Consider decorating or labeling a plain binder to show your personal style, or purchase a decorative binder that makes your heart go pitter-patter. This will help make your diary more enjoyable to reach for as you compile it, as well as more apt to be used.

NEXT, MAKE THE FOLLOWING SECTION LABELS:

- THE ELEMENTS
- SET THE SETTING
- THE SEASONS
- RESOURCES (lined paper)
- MISCELLANEOUS

Put the sections of your binder together and add some plain and lined paper to each, as well as a few of the sheet protectors. With your workbook binder organized and your tools at the ready, you'll begin compiling your Tabletop Diary with the next chapter's installment.

1
The
ELEMENTS
Assembling the Pieces

The process may begin with an *accessory.* Perhaps a bright tablecloth with Technicolor fruits is your inspiration. Then add and subtract pieces as seems fit. Vintage elements— such as a *time-tested* eggbeater and some tea canisters in punchy hues—might make the perfect focal point for your scheme. Items can be serious or *whimsical.* Practical and durable pieces, such as a classic teapot, are always a smart investment for your arranging arsenal. Starting your day with a *treasured* piece, such as a bowl in stop-traffic yellow decorated with a singing gnome, is sure to bring a *smile.* Set it on a French grain sack to show your *personal* style.

ᵒ ABOVE: A whimsical gnome and punchy yellow make this a statement piece.

ᵒ ABOVE RIGHT: Teacups come together with a shared color and period.

ᵒ OPPOSITE, LEFT: This French cast iron teapot by Staub has a classic, rugged look. The French hemp sack adds texture and color.

ᵒ OPPOSITE, RIGHT: Unusual accessories give a tablecloth a personal glow.

Following the lead of whimsical prints and colors, you can throw in other accessories for ornament. You may surprise yourself with this free rein. Even enamel buttons and rolls of ribbon can add interest to a vintage table setting. You can find pizzazz in almost anything, and if it strikes you as beautiful or fun, make room for it at your table.

~ WHAT IS VINTAGE? ~

Vintage pieces are timeless and classic. They are marked by superior character-
istics such as an appealing texture, a bold print, or a particular delicacy, for
example, that of a porcelain tea set. Vintage items have enduring appeal due to
their palatable colors, make, or design. They originate from a past time, usually
at least twenty-five years ago, but their aesthetic value endures beyond the flighty
trends the future will bring. Certain patterns, such as Blue Willow, Royal Stewart
plaid, and designs with flowers as delicate as ribbon are time-tested. Silver, crystal, and china are the mainstays of a well-dressed dining cabinet. If they have

been used from one generation to the next, they will likely be used by future generations. The fact that your vintage ware has an established place in your home testifies to their current appeal.

The use of vintage pieces on today's table can create a deliciously modern feel, just as an Ella Fitzgerald recording piped into the lobby of a hip boutique hotel can sound very "today." Both are distinctive, thus timeless. When mixed with newer pieces in your home, those ever-dependable vintage items will look contemporary. You will discover that combining unlike plates, glasses, and other pieces, perhaps chosen because they share a color or a texture, creates a one-of-a-kind setting that has Vintage Vavoom.

There are more ways to create a vintage table than simply merging period pieces. In fact, you can create a setting exclusively with older pieces while taking a freestyle approach that exudes a twenty-first-century sensibility. For example, rather than following the precision of a traditional table setting, try something different, such as placing shimmery utensils on a chipped-but-still-striking dinner plate or grouping a bouquet of feathers to bloom from a silver chalice. You can create displays either for function (utensils needed for guests) or purely for aesthetic purposes (feathers are hallmarks of a season and add flair to the setting).

Hosting an event offers a perfect opportunity to showcase cupboard favorites; building a tablescape around a distinctive piece is part of the process. A special serving bowl containing pink lemonade can motivate the most reluctant hostess. Her imagination, perhaps sparked by her own childhood memories, gives her inspiration to preside over an unforgettable gathering. Once preparations gain momentum, the chosen theme will become more focused, and appropriate accessories will pop up in a variety of places, from eBay to yard sales to your own attic, closet, or cupboards.

The number of guests you've invited will help determine the extent of your efforts, as will the nature of your gathering. Once you've selected a theme and have finalized the attendees, you will open up your cupboard and interpret its offerings in new ways. Now, get ready—and set!

MAKING
∽ARRANGEMENTS∼

Figuring out how to set all your favorite pieces on the vintage table and still have room for the main course may seem like trying to fit together one of the puzzles you struggled with as a child. By instituting a few changes in your home, you will end up having a better relationship with your possessions.

Simplify your storage process by giving thoughtful consideration to your needs, from everyday use to entertaining. If your closet is so packed that removing one item tips the contents into red alert, this is a signal that it is time for a wardrobe change. Editing your clothing is a therapeutic process. Unloading old garments that match only your hairstyle and shiny red pumps of a decade ago frees space and allows you to dress better—you'll be left with only your best pieces. Editing the contents of your kitchen and dining cabinets is no different.

BELOW: Unexpected items, such as chandelier crystals, play with the light and add interest to the setting.

OPPOSITE: With the ability to see your belongings in *open view,* you can throw in such accents as vintage fruit bowls that will add color and personality to your table.

Your dishware can be organized as tightly as a well-appointed closet. When you're reviewing your home inventory, clump pieces into three categories: save, store, and discard. Arrange your belongings that you decide to keep by color and use. Naturally, your finer items should be stored in a secure place, such as an out-of-reach dining cabinet, shelf, or cupboard designed especially for your best china. Once you winnow your possessions down to your best things, you will be free of clutter and be more able to make use of everything you own. Being organized, in essence, liberates you to be more creative in your tabletop presentations.

Open shelving is encouraged. When your most attractive dishware and accessories are easily visible, you can reflect on their next use as you show them off. Unabashed displays boldly add to a room's style and may inspire you to use pieces that you neglected when they were out of sight.

After determining the nature of the event you are holding—whether casual or formal—the next step is to channel the things you love into your table setting.

Color schemes can never be underestimated as a tool for drawing a tablescape together. While there are many places to find inspiration for an event's color scheme—nature, a favorite painting, a magazine article—your grandmother's handed-down enamelware plates, emblazoned with orange-red roses and bright green leaves against a white background, may in fact provide the color palette that inspires a memorable retro Mother's Day brunch, for example. Your setting might include those plates as well as red-and-white gingham napkins, fresh-mint-sprig-topped iced tea, and a floral arrangement featuring tufts of spring-green wheat grass. Always begin with a strong foundation and build on it.

While the rules for achieving modern vintage style are loose, you can set a rhythm by selecting one primary piece to which you can link additional components. This could be an opulent flower arrangement or a set of ornamental napkin rings that you paid too much for but simply couldn't resist. Mixing and matching is essential to the Vintage

Group like items in *open shelving* that has a neutral palette. When your whims arise, you can add color or other items to help spur the *creative process* that you'll parlay into your tabletop design.

Vavoom process. Vintage and newer pieces go wonderfully together when they share the same color scheme, pattern, or design. Add a variety of levels to your table by using cake plates and pedestal bowls, which literally elevate delicacies and are themselves a treat to the eye. Fill open spaces with such elements as salt and pepper shakers or carafes of wine to keep the spirits flowing—another opportunity for function and style to work together. To avoid ending up with a table that is so crammed that a butter dish gets lost in the hierarchy of more used items, every piece should fill a need as well as add beauty.

When setting the table, you do not have to use pieces from the same set; in fact it is encouraged to incorporate items sourced from a variety of places. This keeps the result from looking like the first social affair a newlywed might hold to showcase her wedding bounty. During your acquisitional sprees, choose items that relate to the pieces you already own. A simple gold pattern on a newer find could unite it with your original set. As your collection grows, there will be more

equations to work with, always an invitation to throw more parties and a chance to dazzle with one-of-a-kind settings.

Displays arranged with motley items acquired from your favorite stores, trips, flea markets, and online auctions honor your personal style as the host. Leave precise table settings to the restaurants—at-home gatherings should be more personal and inviting. You are not only sharing your pieces with your guests but also participating in a ritual that's as revealing as a photo album, an interactive form of intimacy. In short, your gathering is an expression of your personal history and becomes a piece of it. It is essential to entertaining that you become more connected with your guests, in fact. They should not be invited simply to have a good meal and be on their way. A well-set table, laden with your tastefully arranged treasures, creates an opportunity to bond. Conversing about travel, new ideas, and favorite memories fosters closeness and, perhaps, like that age-old kitchen-table "how was your day?" banter, offers a kind of old-fashioned therapy.

∽ An *organized cupboard* not only adds a decorative element to your dining space; having your belongings *attractively* arranged also helps you to become a more creative host.

The
PRINCIPLES

- Simplify your creative process by editing your *storage* facilities.
- Out of sight, out of mind applies when you are not in contact with your tableware. *Open shelving* organizes, and encourages the use of, your favorite pieces.
- Sort your dishware by *categories,* such as color and use.
- Determine the *nature* of your event and number of guests, thereby directing the style of your tabletop.
- Choose a *color palette* or theme to set the table's trend.
- Select an *anchor* piece that becomes a foundation to build on.
- *Mix and match.* Combine vintage items with newer ones, and experiment with different levels and scale.
- Fill open spaces with *ornamental* pieces while keeping in mind that function and beauty should work together.
- Resist the *impulse* to use dishware sourced from only one set.
- Collect pieces that *complement* what you already own.
- *Marrying* together a variety of your things is a chance to show your personal style.
- The ritual of entertaining unites a host with her guests by sharing her most *beloved* possessions in a well-appointed setting.

DESIGNER'S
TOOLKIT

Our distinctive tastes, likes, dislikes, and even memories accompany us on every adventure to a favorite thrift store or flea market. Those preferences propel us to pick up an item or force us to maneuver quickly past it. But once we get our chosen items home, how do we compose tasteful tabletop arrangements?

Each person brings her unique touch to the table—whether she's decorating for an intimate Valentine's Day affair or producing a grand celebration such as a gratitude gathering for friends and colleagues. To start, it's important to know some basic design principles. But breaking the rules and following your heart is just as important for forging your own personal Vintage Vavoom style. Here are some tools for visual design composition as well as some tricks design professionals have learned on the job. These concepts are a base to build upon, not a structure made to stifle. Ultimately, you will trust your ever-flowing ideas and always-growing sense of what works—what feels right to you—to lead you to an inspiring tabletop.

1. COLOR. Just as in nature, cool colors soothe (think sea green, sky blue, fragrant lavender) and hot colors excite or add drama (fire red, sunset orange, lemon yellow). Similar colors used together create harmony—think of the blooms chosen to compose a garden or a combination of hues like cream, brown, and golden yellow. Opposite colors are charged with energy, like a passionate couple. For example, combinations like purple and yellow, which are opposite on the color wheel, will brighten a child's birthday party.

2. TEXTURE. Linens, dishware, and sparkling glasses have a visual chemistry that unites unlike pieces and adds beauty to set a mood.

3. PROPORTION AND SCALE. Rather than look over a flat terrain of basic dishware, variations in height and proportion keep the eye roaming. Pedestal plates and centerpieces are wonderful ways to add to the topography of a well-set table.

4. THE POWER OF THREE. Florists use this principle all the time. While one flower is nice, a group of three is captivating. A tabletop triumvirate need not be limited only to flowers; consider using fruits and elements accrued from nature. The visual interest of an uneven number is exciting, drawing attention to their variety.

5. RHYTHM. As you set your table, there will be a flow that comes naturally. Fall into this creative motion, adding the pieces that connect with your train of thought.

6. BALANCE AND HARMONY. Certain elements will relate to one another no matter how different they may appear. As an example, shelled walnuts and persimmons may seem an unlikely pair, but their colors and interesting textures transform them into a beautiful vignette and may even suggest an overall tabletop scheme.

7. LIGHT AND DARK. Opposites can create drama. Whether you contrast a white charger with a dark table or use candles in a dimly lit room, this technique creates a mood.

8. EMOTIONAL VALUES. Shapes, colors, and textures all evoke emotions. For example, a hard-edged vase is a dominant, more masculine note while the sinuous curve of a teapot is romantic and feminine.

9. LOOKING THROUGH THE LENS. Set the table with an eye to what your guest will see at his or her place.

10. WALKING AWAY FROM THE SHOT. Know when you have created the most wonderful vignette possible and then be able to stand back, breathe, and enjoy your accomplishment.

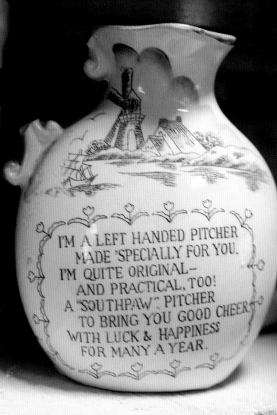

I'M A LEFT HANDED PITCHER
MADE 'SPECIALLY FOR YOU.
I'M QUITE ORIGINAL—
AND PRACTICAL, TOO!
A "SOUTHPAW" PITCHER
TO BRING YOU GOOD CHEER,
WITH LUCK & HAPPINESS
FOR MANY A YEAR.

∽ The first pieces you used as a *child* might be the first pieces in your growing collection, testimony that a tabletop can be your very own vintage-ware *anthology*.

❧ THE PIECES ❧

Dishes, cups, cutlery, glasses, candlesticks, compotes, vases, silver, crystal, linens, and that dish from your childhood that greets you each morning—the list of what you can use for dining is endless, as are the possibilities for their display.

Choosing your dinnerware requires a thoughtful approach because it is a meaningful step in your personal history. Perhaps you'll select pieces for their function and price point, to add a spark of style to a particular celebration or holiday gathering. Or dinnerware can be chosen through the romantic tradition that unites engaged couples—selecting a china pattern, when each learns something new about their beloved from his or her sensibility and taste, and partners share

stories of why a design speaks to them. Perhaps some pieces have been passed down to you, previously used by ancestors in faraway places, and have become mementos of your family's history. From whatever means you acquire your tabletop collection, its elements will likely have an emotional hold on you.

Your tastes and preferences pull on your nostalgia heartstrings. You may unknowingly gravitate toward something that evokes a warm feeling anchored in your past—the dishes that were used at holiday dinners or

ABOVE: Adding *textiles* is another means of giving depth to your vignette. A layering of *fabrics* will show color and style.

OPPOSITE: Once you begin collecting, you may discover that you gravitate toward a *certain feature,* such as color, pattern, or make. Combining like items will create an eye-catching tabletop.

a vase that recalls a special occasion. While visiting the home of a friend whose taste you admire, you could be introduced to new designs, leading to the inevitable question *Wherever did you get such a find?*

Though tastes may change, the creator of the vintage table is typically hard-pressed to let any of her cherished pieces go. She normally makes her acquisitions on an emotional level, harboring the kind of feelings for her possessions that others usually associate with family pets and childhood places. One of the founding principles of Vintage Vavoom style is that when you love something, you will find a place for it.

When acquiring dishware, consider your needs, color scheme, and how well new additions will interact with things you already own. If you are just starting your collection, select pieces that share a similar pattern or period. Acquire the basics, and then, perhaps after your first soiree, add novelty items that will heighten the effectiveness of your table setting at your next gathering. Think of ornamental components—such as compote dishes and pedestal plates—that draw the eye like a finely costumed flamenco dancer on a lonely stage. Weave in linens that play off your arrangement for even more visual impact.

One-of-a-kind *kitchen items*, when grouped together, show personal style.

Before purchasing important pieces, do your research. High-quality china made by luxury brands is assured to be the future generation's heirlooms. If you are hunting for a bargain, trawling for deals on eBay, in thrift stores, at yard sales, or anywhere other than from a tried-and-true vendor, check the item's authenticity before you make the deal. Researching on the Internet will help you learn about your potential acquisition. Or you can befriend an expert to guide you through this important purchase, and have them listed on your speed dial.

No one can resist a one-of-a-kind piece, which sets a vintage table apart from any other. Thus, honing your skills as a true shopping huntress will help you build your unique collection, not to mention provide you with the fun of making thrilling finds!

Along with antiques and vintage pieces, handcrafted items are always a smart investment. There is a wonderful tactile experience that comes from dining with something spun by artistic hands. You can feel the artisan's handprint on every curve, which makes a simple meal more memorable.

⟋ Well-made pieces are certain to be future *heirlooms.*

Dinnerware

From the bowl that holds your morning cereal to the pedestal that showcases Aunt Polly's birthday cake illuminated by ninety-two candles, dishes are the foundation of the table setting. Everyday dishware is like the friend you can count on to make you smile. Used regularly, these pieces are chosen for their ability to weather frequent wear and tear. Nowadays, there's an endless supply of affordable options that don't scrimp on style. They can spark our imagination when we intend to throw together a quick and easy affair.

Your lifestyle determines when you pull out the good china. If your home seems to function as a racetrack for kids and pets, such delicates will be used only on special occasions. Those who enjoy entertaining regularly should use what they love, even if it is very fragile or valuable. Like wearing your best perfume or having a glass of champagne on a random weekday, such indulgences lift the senses.

Dinnerware comes in every variety imaginable. It can be grouped in sets or in compilations of *accrued* finds, all of which become entrusted tools for creating a table's composition.

≈ LEFT: One-of-a-kind pieces are even more *personal* when splashed with your *name*.

≈ OPPOSITE: While many typecast *porcelain* as the delicate pieces tea-drinking grannies favor, it is quite damage-resistant and can last for *generations* if cared for properly.

All the pieces set on a table should perform a function, whether for the proper partaking of the meal or to lend style and beauty. For example, if fish or game is being served, special utensils must be set out. All sorts of accoutrements should accompany a tea, such as strainers for loose leaves, tongs for sugar cubes, and delicate bowls designed especially for clotted cream and jams.

DECIPHERING
DINNERWARE

There are countless options for a place setting with vintage style. Patterns and colors satisfy the eye, but an understanding of how clay is transformed into earthenware, stoneware, porcelain, and bone china will help you prolong the lifespans of your collections. While hunting through flea markets and antique shops or simply when you're looking to arm an entertaining supply closet, it's good to know the differences, qualities, and considerations for each of these four basic ceramics. Here is a guide to help round out your assortments.

EARTHENWARE
BEST FOR: trends, colors, price
HOWEVER: easily breakable

Usually known for its bright, intense colors, earthenware has a substantial and weighty feel. It's best used for casual entertaining and everyday meals. The fact that earthenware is the most porous of dinnerware materials means it's fired at the lowest temperature of all the clays and is also the most brittle. However, the benefits of its quick and inexpensive production process trickle down to the buyer by making earthenware inexpensive—the best choice when buying trendy styles for serving pieces or to update a more classic traditional set at home.

STONEWARE
BEST FOR: casual or everyday dining
HOWEVER: slightly pricier than earthenware

Fired at a higher temperature than earthenware, stoneware is more durable and less prone to scratching and chipping. It has a vitreous, or glassy, quality that makes it more opaque than porcelain, and it is nonporous, making it impervious to liquids. In its natural state, stoneware has a grayish or brownish tint, and it includes some impurities; therefore, it is normally glazed and designed with softer colors.

 When *choosing your china,* be sure to consider its material, what uses it will serve, and its investment potential.

PORCELAIN
BEST FOR: formal dining, durability
HOWEVER: pricey

Porcelain is typically associated with grandmother's delicate teacups; however, this material is actually highly chip-resistant. Along with bone china, it is the most durable dinnerware. With its high firing temperature, high-purity clay, and the addition of kaolin in its production, it has the strength and resilience to shatter any preconceived notions about its fragility. In fact, like bone china, a porcelain teacup is sturdy enough that, when inverted, it can support the weight of an adult human—try it sometime. Kaolin also gives the material its bright whiteness. Thin, dense, and lightweight, these pieces can last lifetimes when they are properly cared for, making them the perfect heirloom. Porcelain should be part of your fine-dining collection.

BONE CHINA
BEST FOR: investment sets
HOWEVER: pricey

As mentioned above, bone china is among the most durable dinnerware materials. Usually designed for elegance and refinement, bone china is the stuff of wedding registries and heirloom collections. It differs from porcelain in that bone ash is added before the firing process occurs (resulting in a slightly creamier color), and it usually has a translucence that allows some light to show through it in direct light.

Utensils

Whether made of heavy pewter or delicate silver, all utensils add shimmer and scale. Beautifully marrying form and function, they are eye-catching enough to become a design element in and of themselves for your tablescape. Set a proper table with your utensils (see page 136) or, for more casual affairs, arrange them like tulips in a vase or clump them in a glass or other intriguing vessel. It's always a good idea to include the entire family of silverware on the table even though your meal may not require certain utensils. You can tie them with twine or lay them facing downward on a pretty embroidered napkin in the European style.

As with everything on the vintage table, imprecision is welcome. An incomplete set amuses the eye with its originality. There is balance from the glimmer. Combine newer pieces with the bone-handled silverware that traveled to this country with your ancestors. A few polished pieces placed softly atop a pretty dish show off the simple beauty of their lines.

∽ TOP: Flatware with mother-of-pearl handles has a timeworn feel.

∽ OPPOSITE, BOTTOM RIGHT: These delicate spoons create a simple beauty and can be used as ornamental pieces on a tablescape.

RIGHT: Glassware doesn't have to be used for its intended purpose. They are dependable vessels for decorative items and can be grouped to create a *sun-glinting vignette.*

OPPOSITE, LEFT: *Mismatched glasses* add interest to a table setting.

OPPOSITE, RIGHT: *Storing* glasses properly helps ensure their life span.

Glassware

Glassware is an elegant addition to any gathering. It is dainty and exquisite, and its simple clear shapes catch light, which bounces onto the other tabletop pieces. Since glassware is held in the hand through much of the duration of a meal, its presence can even have a soothing quality. As many styles and varieties of glasses exist as there were cocktails in the bar car of a train headed toward Connecticut in the 1950s.

A vintage table celebrates the beauty of unlike things grouped together. The neutral elegance of glass is a great unifier, so glassware is the perfect element to employ in creating settings. Kathy Delgado, the proprietress of Los Angeles's Vintageweave Interiors, Inc., specializes in creating beauty through unexpected juxtapositions. Her store is an emporium of varied items, showcasing ideas in every available space. "The traditional method of using glass dinnerware is to collect all one pattern. However, for a more unique, modern approach, I like

to mix up the patterns of any clear glass for added interest. For instance, for one setting, the water glasses will be Fostoria Americana goblets, and another pattern will serve as the wineglasses, and so on," Kathy says. "Don't be limited by using each glass only for its originally intended purpose. I will often set up four glasses at each place setting, and each vintage glass was used as a wineglass originally."

Kathy collects clear glass such as the simple baker's pedestal cake plate, and uses it alongside an intricately cut glass of the Depression style, Fostoria Americana, and the antique pattern Pleat and Panel. "My favorite decorating tools are pedestal plates. They are used to showcase bowls and platters of food to add interesting heights to a buffet table. Since candles are mainstays of any gathering, my favorite visual trick is to stack them in trios on pedestal plates all over the home and down the center of the farmhouse table. It lifts the candles off the table and puts them in a more face-flattering height. Rarely do my pedestal cake plates hold actual cakes," Kathy says.

THE RIGHT
PRESCRIPTION

Here is a glossary of those glasses every good hostess should have:

- SHORT TUMBLER: A shorter glass used for juice, water, whiskey, or soda, with the capacity to contain 5 to 6 ounces of liquid.
- WATER GLASS: A straight, larger glass used for fruity mixed drinks, soda, iced tea, or water, with the capacity to contain 10 to 12 ounces of liquid.
- GOBLET: Originally designed for water, this shrunken wineglass is an elegant addition to a more formal setting, with the capacity to contain 6 to 12 ounces of liquid.
- WINEGLASS (FOR WHITE WINE): Choose wineglasses that can accommodate 8 to 12 ounces of liquid. You want the glass to be large enough to hold a full serving without reaching halfway full.
- WINEGLASS (FOR RED WINE): With a fatter tulip bowl than the white wineglass, this glass is designed to heighten the sensory experience of drinking red wine.
- COCKTAIL OR MARTINI GLASS: With its reversed-flying-saucer top, it makes a great presentation for martinis, margaritas, cosmopolitans, and mixed cocktails and has the capacity to hold 4 to 12 ounces. Although a variety of glasses can be used to contain the many concoctions bartenders have created over the years (like a straight-sided Collins glass, which holds about 14 ounces) the classic martini glass, or cocktail glass, works well for many different drinks.
- CHAMPAGNE SAUCER OR COUPE: A vintage style that is not as popular for serving champagne today because the wide top allows the bubbly's bouquet to escape, this is a smaller, rounded version of the cocktail glass, and it can be used similarly. It holds a 3- to 5-ounce cocktail or champagne and works well for sherbet and seafood cocktails too.
- FLUTE: With its tall and sexy shape, this svelte piece is used for champagne, champagne cocktails, and sparkling wine, with the capacity to contain 4 ounces of liquid.

- CORDIAL OR LIQUEUR: Approximately 4 inches tall, this petite stemware holds about 2 ounces of liquid.
- SHOT GLASS: This tiny glass—commonly associated with inexpensive airport souvenirs—is used for drinking or measuring shots of hard liquor, with the capacity to contain 1 to 2 ounces of liquid.

CARING FOR STEMWARE

- Eschew the dishwasher and hand wash these delicate pieces with hot water and a little detergent.
- Rinse glassware in hot water to assist in the drying process (the water evaporates more quickly), and finish by gently hand drying it with a nonabrasive dish towel or lint-free cloth.
- Store glasses upright in a well-ventilated cupboard or on a shelf or a special rack designed for them.

Linens

The function of linens is to provide color and texture to the table while also indicating the theme and formality of the gathering. You can dress up your setting with a tablecloth, runner, and swatches of lace or simple place mats. Choose coverings from among the infinite colorful patterns available, to make the table pop, or mark an elegant affair with classic linen. For example, fine Irish linen will dictate elegance, while a layering of antique grain sacks will not only show an original use of textiles but also signal a more casual affair. Linens should be chosen for their quality and design and be made with natural materials such as cotton. Check its seams to see how the piece was created. Handmade pieces are excellent additions.

If your event is seated instead of buffet-style, as a rule, tablecloths should not fall to the ground, since guests need to easily navigate to and from their chairs. Also, consider forgoing tablecloths altogether to show the beauty of a surface, such as shimmery mahogany or simple, subtly colored marble. Warm up the setting with coverlets and, naturally, your pieces will beautifully cover the terrain.

The rugged good looks of classic linens, in patterns that simplify the palette, set the foundation for a well-appointed table.

Linen napkins provide another opportunity to weave color and design into your setting. Paper napkins should be used only if they are attractive or create a retro feel. Otherwise, save the expense—and our natural resources—by using cotton or linen styles. Even heavy dishcloths in fun designs can attractively add to your table. It is not necessary to use sturdy linens just for drying dishes. In a pinch, they serve excellently as napkins, trivets, place mats, or in an assembly of different dishcloths to create a patchwork tablecloth that is both inventive and practical.

ABOVE RIGHT: A variety of colorful towels punch up the color scheme. ABOVE LEFT AND BELOW RIGHT: Wrapped in a ribbon, the most fundamental textile is beautiful. BELOW LEFT: Delicate lace overlaying a weathered wood table refines an otherwise informal setting. OPPOSITE: Embroidered napkins add a pinch of color and personality to an otherwise neutral table.

~ABOVE: A handmade pincushion perched atop vibrant towels shows the whimsy and animated flair of a bold host. ~ABOVE RIGHT: Always treat your *linens* with care, and read washing *instructions* on their labels. ~RIGHT: Personal family portraits invite spirited discussion, while the neutral sepia tones add interest to the table.

~OPPOSITE, LEFT: Don't fret that *heirloom* linens are too nice to use; they were created to endure.

~OPPOSITE, RIGHT: Lightly scented fragrance sticks create a soothing environment.

Caring for Linens

Fine linens are an investment and should be treated as such. However, you should not be wary of using them. Why have beautiful things if they are only admired from afar? Enjoy your pretties, and care for them so they can be used for generations to come.

Wash your linens by following their instruction labels. Use a gentle cleanser such as Ivory Snow, a special linen detergent, or natural ingredients, and use sparingly. Even if a piece is machine washable, evaluate it in its entirety before tossing it in the machine to see if there are any stains that should be spot treated before a washing sets the blemish even deeper. Avoid mixing your fine linens

with other laundry items, as these keepsakes should be spared any potential hazards outside elements might cause. Remove the laundered pieces immediately from the washer and shake them, which will prevent wrinkling or damp odors from setting in. Air-drying is preferred over the abrasive tumble of a machine dryer. The sun is a natural bleaching agent, which should be noted if you do not want to fade colorful items. Take caution when ironing. Always make sure the iron's temperature is properly set and that the iron and ironing board cover are clean. Placing a white handkerchief or light sheet over the linen while ironing will help prevent scorch marks. If you do burn the cloth, dab the mark with a mixture of cool water and peroxide. If the burn is too severe, take the piece to your trusted tailor, who can mend it. Baking soda, white distilled vinegar, salt, seltzer, and lemon juice are other safe ingredients for removing stains from your fineries.

↪ LEFT: In selecting your linens, experiment with different textures and patterns.

↪ OPPOSITE: Create an inspiration board of favorite swatches to spark your next tabletop design.

Repair fine linens carefully. Mend severe damage such as tears or permanent stains with embellishments such as ribbon and colorful trimmings.

Store laundered linens in a ventilated place with cloth sachets. Resist the temptation to intersperse sprigs of dried lavender or rose in direct contact with the items, as they can stain them, but cloth sachets filled with dried lavender work well to repel pests. Cedar blocks are ineffective when their odor diminishes, so if needed, lightly sand the blocks to bring back their useful scent. Do not use mothballs, which are toxic, not to mention that they exude a stomach-churning odor. Use your linens in rotation to keep each item equally preserved. If these are investment pieces, take them out to use on occasion, perhaps draping another linen atop them for protection. Or finish your linens' surface with a stain-resisting spray such as Scotchgard. While such treatment may diminish a piece's value, it will enable you to use your best items and may extend their lives by protecting them against moisture.

~ABOVE: From preparing the meal to setting the table, put vintage *kitchen items* to good use by using them every day. ~ABOVE RIGHT: Colorful *kitchen towels* add whimsy. ~ BELOW: The nostalgic feel of kitchen collectibles is always in vogue. ~OPPOSITE: Simple, *well-made* pieces are the go-to treasured objects that dependably contribute to your table setting.

Retro Active

Returning to the ritual of family dinners conjures up a hospitable feeling worthy of the comfort food you might serve. Period kitchen collectibles are major objects of desire among history hunters. Just try bidding on a pristine blue enamel kettle on eBay and you'll connect with legions of devotees. Categories in this ever-growing field include Pyrex, Depression glass, vintage kitchen utensils, cookie jars, tea towels, appliances, cookbooks, and just about anything that reminds you of preparing family dinners from scratch. Such collectibles often have tones and patterns reminiscent of Carmen Miranda's fruit bowl of a hat, shades that are nostalgic and inviting, and are just as durable now as they were when they were first used.

Vignettes and settings built around vintage kitchen collectibles mix well together because they are unique items that all come with a story—table-setting history at its best. Newer pieces in vintage styles are widely available. Many of today's pieces are made well, with unique designs inspired by classic pieces, and designers often create them this way so that they are destined to be the next collectible. Dining with these dependable items every day turns that six P.M. dinnertime into a hard appointment to break.

A BRIEF HISTORY OF KITCHEN COLLECTIBLES

Wait before tossing out that measuring cup or Tupperware canister; your ordinary kitchen necessities may be tomorrow's treasures. Just look at how Jadite dishes throw in punches of sea foam green on the trendiest tables today. These pieces, which date back to the 1940s, are from Fire-King—a brand made by Anchor Hocking, a company known for glassware, which is still in production today. The sets range from plates to salt and pepper shakers and were intended for everyday use. They were available as promotional pieces—sold in flour bags or as premiums at hardware stores and gas stations—and could be bought at five-and-dime stores and supermarkets. Jadite also comes in white, pink, and all spectrums of blue. Collecting Fire-King pieces has become a growing trend, owing to their fashionable colors, durability, and ability to provide a dependably strong accent in a true vintage cottage kitchen.

Other collectibles worth keeping an eye out for include aprons, linens, melon ballers, rolling pins, choppers, beaters, measuring scales, pizza cutters, can openers, and crimpers, those nifty gadgets that spiffed up Aunt Molly's piecrusts. With such a wide collecting field, prices can be quite reasonable. You could collect based on color, theme, or specific function, such as with match safes, which you might display on the wall, typically next to the stove. Small decorative tins, match safes were made to hold wooden matches and were usually hung near the stove at a time when the strike of a match was needed to start cooking. They can sell for twenty-five to forty dollars. As a rule, condition and rarity determine prices with any collectible, and the more original the condition of your match safe, the higher its value. While these modest items can still perform vigorously despite their age, they also serve as a unique design element that adds interest to your table and kitchen vignettes.

FURNESS

DAVIS

HUMFR... COMPLETE COOK BOOK

ZEL ...ER'S ...EEZER OOK OK

the Cook is in the Parlor

M'CARTHY

Westinghouse COOK BOOK prepared by Julia Kiene

LET'S COOK IT RIGHT

LILY HAXWORTH WALLACE

THE AMERICAN WOMAN'S COOK BOOK

NATIONAL BINDING

SALT

PEPP

Displaying your collectibles openly is a way to admire them every day and encourage frequent use.

∽ *Ladurée* chocolates and delights are handsomely packaged. Their *mint tone* with its hints of gold lends a sophisticated ice cream parlor feel, a wonderful accent to your table setting.

∼ACCENTS∽

Once a table is properly set, all the important pieces in place, the moment arrives when a host can truly shine. The vintage table is a theatrical one, and if the dishware is the cast, accents are the song-and-dance sequence. They dazzle, move the drama along at toe-tapping speed, and offer a feast for the eyes.

Choose accessories based on need. Salt and pepper shakers, embroidered linens, butter dishes, and that gravy boat that may be used just once a year are embellishments. Again, this is a time to be creative, so your pieces do not have to come from a matching set. In fact, whimsy is encouraged. Vintage bowls come in a dizzying array of shapes and sizes, from divided glass bowls shaped like four-leaf clovers to diminutive footed china finger bowls. Use such frivolous pieces to serve condiments, or float delicate flowers in them at each place setting. Flowers are dependable centerpieces, of course. Introducing unusual vessels like a blue

mason jar, a small tin watering can, or a jar inside of a vintage seed box can bring charm to the setting. Or think outside the standard florals to create centerpieces from food and other delicacies. Fans interspersed with paper butterflies add a fanciful touch while allowing guests an old-fashioned means of finding relief from summer's heat.

Your table is the stage. Theater sets can be filled with embellishments or they can be sparse and evocative. A table setting is no different. Be fanciful. Look to packaging, the colors in fashion, and the produce aisle in your local supermarket to see the season's stars on display, all of which can be inspirations for your table-top display. Weave shiny ribbons and handsomely packaged chocolates aside plates and water glasses. Sachets with embroidered sentiments always arouse the senses. Hand-crocheted items your ancestors created are nice personal touches. The combinations are endless, and you are the author of the rules.

LEFT: On hotter days provide guests with a fan, another example of style paired with function.

BELOW AND OPPOSITE: Rolls of vintage ribbon inspire with color and offer embellishment for your setting.

Place Cards

These delicate little pieces are loaded with implications. A good hostess understands the importance of the seating plan. Potential flare-ups can be avoided or a romance may blossom, all due to the seating arrangement. Before guests congregate at the table, they will peek at the setting and immediately focus on the place cards, searching for their name with anticipation.

When following the rules of etiquette, the host should always be seated at the head of the table, typically near the entrance to the kitchen. A female guest of honor sits to the host's right, and a male guest of honor to the host's left. It is customary to pair male and female guests aside each other.

For larger affairs, arrange tables so that each appears to be a worthy place to sit. The lone table dangling at the edge of the room is an easy mark as the last-minute-invitee setting and is certain to sour the moods of those dining there. Be sure to mix up the guests. Match personalities and shared interests rather than creating the oh-so-obvious singles and married-couple tables or common age groups. However, if there are enough children to form their own table, kiddies will appreciate breaking from parents as much as the adults will enjoy their grown-up time. Of course, moving cards after your guests have arrived is a definite no-no.

Place cards are not exclusive to formal gatherings. They are helpful in alleviating an uncomfortable moment for a bashful guest, whether at a six-year-old's birthday party or a soiree with a royal guest list. Place cards can be whimsical devices, a perfect accessory to fill a table's vacant space, showcasing witty words or language from a favorite storybook that sets the theme of the affair.

In addition to traditional tented cards made from heavy stock paper, you can choose from a variety of offerings. Wedding-favor websites are jammed with enticing alternatives. You can even be creative and design your own. Lean the cards against seashells or favorite collectibles such as snow globes. Nestle them in small spotted plants. Slice a piece of citrus fruit into wedges and score small slits in the rinds to hold the cards. The possibilities abound.

Mangez moi
Buvez moi

~ ABOVE: *Place card* holders do all the talking. These little pieces can save a lot of aggravation.

~ ABOVE RIGHT: Lines taken from *Alice in Wonderland*'s tea party amuse guests and create a storybook atmosphere.

~ RIGHT: A good host must know how to set the table properly. Then she can set out on her own to add some *fun and flair.*

Flowers have many *personalities*. Roses, with their *elegance*, are always an easy pleaser, while more unusual blooms can wow, since they deviate from the expected. When selecting flowers, *color and texture* should be emphasized. Even a selection of three unlike blooms can become united, resulting in an arrangement as unique as your tabletop style.

Flowers

Opulent blooms with accent flowers that drip like crystals, or buds pulled from the garden can serve as the basis for a table's scheme. What is happening outdoors will intimately influence your choices.

Follow the lead of top florists, those genius designers who have the power to determine the date of a celebrity wedding based on *their* schedule. While their talent is partly instinctual, floral professionals are acutely sensitive to the seasons and what fresh offerings are available, not just flowers but also fruits, vegetables, and other seasonal delights that will mix well with robust blossoms.

When deciding on your arrangement, consider matching blooms to your tableware, accent pieces, and color scheme. The scale of the event will also influence your selection. It can be a simple arrangement of just one flower or sections of three unlike colors that culminate in a dazzling spectacle of vivid tones and textures. Day-opened roses in an elegant silver vase are always a harbinger of easy romantic style, while gerbera daisies in luscious colors look as friendly as a Labrador puppy. Whatever kind you choose, flowers are an essential element to the vintage table.

Shop your florist, farmers' market, or even your grocery store to see which blooms are available. Such inspiration can determine the nature of your affair.

～ FLORAL ～
CONSIDERATIONS

Amanda Heer, *Romantic Homes* magazine contributor and designer of Fantasy Florals, offers her following secrets to creating great flower displays:

1. WORK WITHIN THE THEME and feel of your event, whether it is a simple dinner party or something on a larger scale.

2. Try not to overthink your arrangement for a dinner party. KEEP IT SIMPLE to create a statement.

3. Try three TONES OF FLOWERS or other organics in different textures. As an example, papery hydrangeas, velvety roses, and smooth coffee beans create a beautiful medley.

4. Since seasons come and go so quickly, use shades that have year-round appeal, then embellish with TRADITIONAL holiday touches for a twist.

5. Buy what is in SEASON.

6. Look for tight blooms, and CHECK THE BASE OF THE STEMS before buying. Make sure they are tight and fresh cut. Always check the leaves on the blooms, they should be firm and bright green.

7. Work with NEW AND UNUSUAL shades of flowers massed together for greater impact.

8. CONTAINERS can become the inspiration or set the color. Keep an open mind, as you do not have to use a traditional vase as your container. Line a porous container with an extra-large ziplock baggie to make it water-tight.

9. EXPERIMENT with using just one shade as a theme. For example, arrange all orange flowers in one vase and sunken kumquats and floating candles in another. Other interesting combinations are red roses and cranberries, yellow tulips and lemons, green roses and limes—peruse the produce section for fresh inspiration.

10. If you are on a BUDGET, fill a shallow vessel with water and float the heads of flowers and clusters of votives for impact. Other ideas include using apple slices or other seasonal fruits, which can be displayed atop a fun tablecloth or runner for personal style.

11. Fill glass vases with ROSE PETALS.

12. CANDLESCAPES are becoming more popular and add drama when grouped alongside flowers.

LOOKS GOOD ON
⁓PAPER⁓

For her wedding, *Romantic Homes* senior editor Jickie Torres left the flowers in the fields and opted for paper creations to brighten her tabletop. This unique look is reflective of Jickie's signature style, and guests were dazzled by the colorful additions that were almost as lovely as the bride.

Paper flower–making is a domestic art form in many cultures. In ancient China, colorful paper was folded into flower shapes and set upon pools of water as offerings to ancestors. In Renaissance Italy, colorful paper flowers were created for festivals, and the bright custom soon made its way to France, where artists were already fashioning papier-mâché blooms. In Latin America, tissue paper is constructed into flower garlands throughout the year as al fresco decor and is especially prevalent each November for the *Día de los Muertos* (Day of the Dead) festival, just before Halloween.

Incorporating paper flowers into your entertaining is both whimsical and modern. Create an entire bouquet or incorporate a single bloom into a bevy of fresh flowers for a surprise. Here are a few of Jickie's tips on making faux florals.

- SEARCH ONLINE to find ready-made patterns for simple blooms. You'll often find these on classroom-project sites or cultural history sites. Once you've practiced on a few samples, you can use this basic knowledge to figure out how to construct more complicated specimens.
- TISSUE PAPER is best for full, densely layered flowers such as carnations and chrysanthemums. Crepe paper is dense and moldable, making it perfect for simple structural blooms such as tulips and irises or for flowers with specific silhouettes, such as peonies and roses.
- Browse the FLORAL SUPPLIES section of your crafts store. You'll need floral wire for the stem and floral tape for adhering leaves and petals and for wrapping around the wire stem to achieve a softer look.
- Some varieties, such as peonies and hibiscus, will benefit from a dab of HOT GLUE along the sides, as their oversized leaves may otherwise hang too low.
- Once done, keep flowers out of HUMID areas, where moisture in the air can cause the paper to bleed or droop.
- Take chances on VIVID COLORS and overscale flowers for a fun, bright look. Go for small floral bouquets in more natural colors for a more elegant setting.

DO IT YOURSELF
INSTRUCTIONS FOR PAPER PEONIES

1. Peonies have an almost egg-shaped petal that is slightly fringed at the top. Using patterns based on the images above, trace petal shapes onto crepe paper. Place each petal pattern so that the paper grain is vertical—this allows you to spread and stretch the petal as needed.

2. Cut petal shapes in three sizes: small, medium, and large. No need to be too precise here. Pull each petal slightly from each side to spread open the grain. This will result in a cupped shape, giving the paper the natural look of a petal.

3. To prepare the stem and stamens, cut a standard length of floral wire in half. Using yellow construction paper or scrapbook paper, cut out a one-by-two-inch rectangle. Fold it in half width-wise, and make cuts all along the top edges, fraying the paper to form the stamens. Cut a half-inch slit into each side of the folded crease (you will use the middle portion to anchor the stamens to the wire). Bend the top three inches of the floral wire into a U shape and slide the U-bend over the middle portion of the fold of the paper stamens. Twist the wire around to secure the paper in place. Roll the fringed paper into a tube, tape in place and separate the frays slightly to give the appearance of stamens.

4. Use the small petal cut-outs to form the first row of petals, orienting the fat side of the petal at the top. Surround the stamens with about four petals, overlapping each petal as you go. Hold the petals in place while you wrap floral tape around the base of the stamens to stick the petals into place. Wrap any excess floral tape tightly around the wire, easing it down toward the end of the stem.

5. Repeat with each petal size, forming two rows of the medium petals and two rows of the large petals, wrapping excess floral tape down along the stem. You may need to hot-glue the petals in certain key spots at their base and midway up the petal for the larger sizes. This keeps the paper from bending backward and still allows the peony to hold its fluffy, ruffled shape.

Edibles

With all this attention to the table setting, the little matter of what to eat should not be an afterthought. What you serve should be more than just a meal to satisfy, and it should be worthy of the environment you are creating. Even breakfast can be an opportunity to create an eye-catching table. A satisfying bowl of oatmeal, for instance, can be adorned with drizzles of glistening honey and an array of cinnamon sticks for a heightened experience. Fine cheeses so aesthetically arranged that they could be the subject of a Flemish painter's still life, a bowl of Granny Smith apples that adds a jolt of color to a neutral table—these are little ways your work at the tabletop is like an artist's efforts on a masterpiece. Chocolate bars wrapped in interesting paper appear like little gifts. A ladylike tea is always an opportunity to showcase the prettiest little delectables of a storybook variety. The spectacle is intensified with meringues that taste like little clouds, bite-sized tarts accented with sugared candies, chocolates worthy of an exhibition, and

other sweets galore that raise a pastry chef's culinary inventiveness to the level of fine art. As with your flower arrangement, the menu should be selected based on what is happening outdoors. Freshness, the seasonal palette, and the nature of the fete will naturally determine the courses.

Creating your menu can be as easy as baking your one tried-and-true dish and then dolling it up in the manner of a restaurant with a monthlong waiting list. Accent each plate with sprigs of herbs or an artful swish of a colorful sauce. There is another secret recipe a good hostess commonly employs: trusting in her favorite bakery or specialty foods shop. Even your supermarket has aisles

ABOVE LEFT: This decadent chocolate cake is dramatized when displayed on a cake stand. The added height adds intrigue to the roaming eye.

ABOVE RIGHT: Handsomely packaged chocolate bars make a style statement when set on their own.

OPPOSITE, LEFT: A stack of *Hermès boxes* props up a delightful bowl.

OPPOSITE, RIGHT: Miniature *delicacies* are like madcap heroines from the silver screen of yesteryear.

devoted to edible pretties, a real time and stress saver, since all you need do is correctly time the moment to open the box. If you love to cook, preparing your favorite dishes and presenting them on the table you created is the truest form of sharing with your guests. Keep it fun and easy so that you can be a guest at your own party.

Edibles need not be eaten. Nature's best offerings visually sing on the table. For instance, pomegranates cut in half and showcased on a gold pedestal look like high art. Stemmed kumquats, pears, lemons, and persimmons all have interesting shapes and colors. A neutral palette is given the designer treatment when paired with contrasting vivid fruits and vegetables. Either create a centerpiece with edibles or simply place some here and there.

Sometimes your collectibles can dictate your table ornamentation. For example, why not intersperse actual oranges with juice glasses printed with Florida's favorite fruit? Fruits and vegetables have long been the subject of prints and art, thus they are ripe for employment in your tabletop arrangements.

RIGHT: There are basic *cakes,* and some that put all others to shame. OPPOSITE: Cinnamon ribbon candy has a Candy Land feel from its curvy texture, retro appeal, and color.

LEFT: Candelabras are always statement pieces; add a vintage base and freshly picked blooms for more drama.

OPPOSITE: *Candles* can perform in a pinch; they are a dependable contribution to a well-thought-out setting.

Candles

To be caught in the flicker of candlelight is like being eyed by a skilled seductress. The soft, natural lighting reveals the same subtle mood as a come-hither glance. These simple accoutrements heighten the most basic table scheme. Simple votives dotted in the middle of a table show personal style, while extravagant candelabras possess easy lavishness. Candles and silver have a relationship that's classic—think Ginger and Fred. Candelabras bring in instant, dramatic beauty.

Consider using pillars in a variety of sizes to add scale. From their thick shapes to their simple utilitarian feel, they bring a contemporary romantic note to your vintage setting. Either cluster them in the middle of the table, perhaps on an old platter, or scatter them here and there. Effortless romance is achieved with the natural light that only a match and a candlestick can produce.

BELOW LEFT AND RIGHT: You can always use a little color. Dishes, tablecloths, and what you serve become a *retro kaleidoscope*.

BOTTOM: Choose a few colors, such as lavender and pink, as the base of your theme. Then throw in details for *impact*.

～ COLOR <u>AND</u> SCALE ～

Color is the go-to accent to make eyes widen, to soothe, or to excite. Your color scheme will help determine the style of your table. You can base your palette on elements ranging from the trim on your dishware to the print on the tablecloth or your selection of flowers. The scheme can be a single color or a grouping of different hues that reflect current trends. In any combination, color is the cream-in-the-middle delight that causes tummies to flip.

A table bursting with color is vivacious, engaging, and as cheerful as a polka-dotted toadstool. If employing a colorful scheme with multiple hues, be sure to link all the chosen colors so they don't look like a child's first drawing created with a box of Crayolas. In the same way you use a variety of flowers in your garden, an overall seamless look in the way colors are grouped should be your aim. For example, you can harmoniously unite five or more hues in a pastel scheme. Resist using too many unlike colors, as the juxtaposition may be overwhelming. You can also use this opportunity to integrate a variety of pieces with a common thread. If you acquired your dishes based on what appeals to you, there is a strong likelihood that most of your purchases will have a unified feel. Once you choose the dishes, cake plates, and other items needed for your setting, throw in accents that will surprise and pop. Paper umbrellas, striped cushion seats, linens, festive aprons, and flowers animate a table and add to its visual composition. What you serve can also participate in this colorful brigade. Citrus fruits can garnish your drinks and contribute a bolt of color to the tablescape. A basic Bundt cake can be spruced up with a pot of edible flowers arranged in the middle. Jelly beans need not wait till the Easter bunny comes to town, as a bowl filled with these colorful gems offers literal eye candy. Cakes, hot chocolate with a head of whipped cream and sprinkles, and retro candy popping from festive dishware or spotlighted on a pedestal dish add a flavorful punch. Enjoying a bowl of mint-chocolate-chip ice cream in this Candy Land ambience takes you back to childhood. The process of infusing your table with color is fun, the free range is liberating, and the results are delicious.

ABOVE AND OPPOSITE, TOP: Color is the detail that takes a table from pretty to drop-dead gorgeous. ABOVE RIGHT: This stack of plates by Vietri looks fantastic without a tablecloth because of the vibrant green hue. BELOW: Fabrics and *textiles* offer colorful visual contrast. BELOW RIGHT: Use many fanciful details that relate to your color scheme on the table, such as tea canisters and jelly beans, which delight the eye and the palate. OPPOSITE, BELOW: Consider what you serve as accessories to a colorful wardrobe. Here, pistachio ice cream adds to the play on color.

Setting the Palette

Today's color choices for the vintage table are as plentiful as paint chips. Black, gold, and silver are always elegant hues and are as modern today as they were in the Art Deco and early Hollywood silver screen periods, when they truly reigned. Gentle colors such as pistachio and rose, paired with soft linens and pink-tinted glassware, evoke a warmer climate and create a lighthearted gathering. Some colors will always be safe, such as white and neutrals, while bold colors show pizzazz and a bit of risk-taking. Deep purple and orange are gutsy and fun, destined to make an impact. You may find that creating unlikely pairings becomes your signature on the vintage-styled table. Perhaps you've always been a fan of raspberry and gold and, when you find pieces in those hues on your hunts, you are quick to snatch them up, knowing that they will certainly get along nicely with your other pieces.

Dishware need not be of the colorful variety to add personal style. All-white china is a trusted choice for its versatility and its ability to provide a reliable foundation for a colorful table. An alternative to using colorful accents is to integrate one dominant color that has a significant impact when cast alongside a white palette.

BOLD AND BEAUTIFUL

Bold-faced items are not restricted to the gossip columns. And, as anyone will tell you, putting something in print is a sure way to get a reaction. Letters have a charm and style that add vavoom to your table's vignettes. Designer Cary Nowell is the consummate letter writer. She creates cone-shaped pots, dishes, and platters with numbers, letters, and stripes for this signature look. The classic black-and-white tone is modern yet reminiscent of classic newsprint. Statement pieces with these timeless prints serve as great conversation starters.

Weave in touches of metallic, such as a table mat woven with golden thread, and prop your ornamental black pieces on the nifty box they came in for a modern gothic style. Unconventional accents, like a black globe or silver antique pheasants, will surprise and delight guests.

∽ OPPOSITE: *Words* are always a powerful communicator. ∽ TOP LEFT AND RIGHT: The graphic look of a *classic letter* is decidedly modern, from its simplicity to its scale. ∽ CLOCKWISE FROM MIDDLE RIGHT: Black and white is an elegant stabilizer for a setting. Mix in *metallic* hues, either with textural paper or interesting *silver* pieces, for a uniquely styled vignette.

THE ELEMENTS

Using what you've learned, gather your thoughts—and pieces—to organize your next event. Devote an afternoon entirely to taking an inventory of the things you already own, do some thoughtful editing, and then consider what additions you would like to include.

In your trusted binder, assemble your ideas and document your design process. This will build on your personal style. Create the following:

1. AN INVENTORY OF YOUR DISHWARE AND VINTAGE TABLE ELEMENTS. Set all of the pieces in clear view on a large kitchen or dining room table, organized by type of piece, color, and preference. Note which pieces you regularly use and which go underappreciated. Some items may need to be placed in storage to make room for your future needs and to avoid overwhelming clutter. Be careful not to throw anything out that makes you hesitate to do so—those pieces may return to your favor.

2. ONCE YOUR ORGANIZING PROCESS IS COMPLETE, SEE IF A THEME OR TREND EMERGES. Perhaps a particular color dominates or it becomes clear that a period has captured your interest. Take digital snapshots and bring the images with you the next time you visit the bakery or a flea market—or any place that can provide additional elements for the theme of your next gathering.

3. CLEAN YOUR STORAGE FACILITIES AND THEN RETURN YOUR PIECES TO THEM. Keep changing their positions around until you have it just right. This is a never-ending process, as shifting items is a constant way to freshen the look.

Now that your pieces are in place and stored in an organized fashion, you will be more inclined to create a table with Vintage Vavoom on a more regular basis.

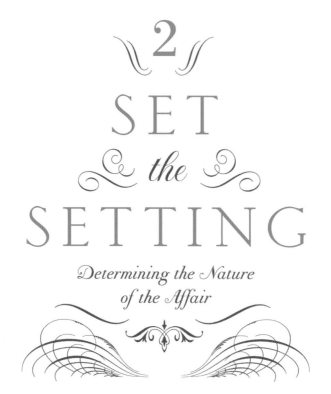

2

SET
the
SETTING

*Determining the Nature
of the Affair*

When planning an affair, begin by determining the *nature of the event.* Is it a simple family gathering, or something more lavish to commemorate a *milestone* event? You might even take this opportunity to christen your new *Spode* dishware that you purchased for a song at a *consignment* shop. Whatever the cause for celebration, your chosen theme will direct the table setting.

⌒ RIGHT: Warmer seasons always call for entertaining outdoors. Weave in indoor elements for a more comfortable surrounding.

⌒ OPPOSITE, LEFT: The punchy toile pattern of this place mat aptly corresponds to these serving pieces by Le Sabre as they all share the theme of color.

⌒ OPPOSITE, RIGHT: Wine given in a fun tote is a reliable hostess gift.

⌒ PRECEDING PAGE: Just as you would want to avoid overdressing for a casual party, be careful not to create an overdone setting that is at odds with the easy nature of the event.

A common mistake hostesses make is trying to tackle too much in too short a period of time, which can sour the enjoyment of creating the vintage table. Be reasonable with your deadlines and goals. Use the pieces you already have to realize a setting you can be happy with, then, if time permits, add the extra, special touches.

Your choice of location is important in determining the ambience and nature of the function, and careful planning will ensure that you, as the hostess, enjoy the party as much as your guests do. Select your settings by keeping function and style in play. For example, if you decide to host your party outdoors, be sure that your tables are in close proximity to the kitchen, or use a table setting that is easily maneuverable from indoors to outdoors, and vice versa, for easy cleanup. Trays are always valued assistants for transporting your table arrangements and food. Also consider placing a lined basket beneath your serving table for collecting rubbish.

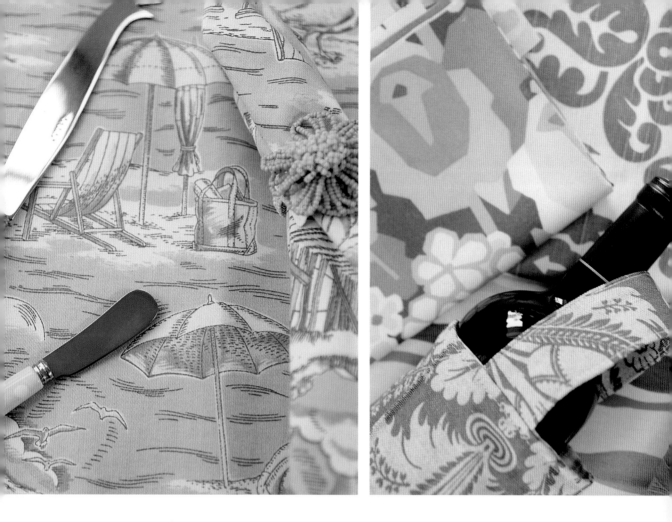

Since the outdoors fosters a more casual affair, be looser in the table arrangements, and call upon dishware so sturdy that there is no need for place mats. The menu can also be seasonally inspired, such as a block of cheese accented by seasonal berries. A wrought-iron chandelier festooned with lilies dropping from the beam of a caravan or a lavish centerpiece of edible fruits adds the right balance between drama and function. Flowers always add beauty, even when—perhaps especially when—they are as simple as wild blooms potted in a galvanized tin. Or consider a carefree arrangement of lemons, for colorful accents.

For simple indoor affairs, forgo high-maintenance linens for the raw look of a wooden or glass tabletop. Remnants of washable fabrics, layered with European grain sacks, offer an organic style while also injecting a color scheme that will set the overall palette.

Once you are fully in hostess mode, you'll find that your guests linger longer than you anticipated. The pleasure you derive from these occasions will make you want to keep your apron on duty through-out the year. As for being a guest who can be assured future invites, dazzle with your enthusiasm, show your personality by shar-ing stories that invite giggles, and keep in mind that it is polite to give your host a gift—always appreciated—such as a one-of-a-kind canvas tote packed with wine.

↝ ABOVE LEFT: There is no need to overdo your next affair. In fact, forgo a pricey florist and use *flowers* you already have in your *garden.*

↝ ABOVE RIGHT: *Fruit and food* are pleasing additions to the tabletop.

↝ OPPOSITE: A trio of aprons entices the always-working hostess, so pretty they look fantastic over her cocktail attire.

∽ THIS PAGE: A *cozy kitchen* becomes a welcome place for daily family gatherings. ∽ OPPOSITE: Pieces that recall *Europe* lend beauty to a vintage table.

∽ALL IN THE FAMILY∽

You do not have to wait for an affair with invited guests to set the table with style. In fact, you can use your creativity every day, with family members as the celebratory participants. Shared meals are a welcome luxury in today's household, which often serves more as a way station between manic activities than as a relaxing oasis. Back when station wagons were guzzling gas, those prototypical happy families who once honored six P.M. dinners may be able to attribute their abiding sense of goodwill to those mealtime gatherings.

Family-style meals always make for an easy affair. Large portions set on platters in the middle of the table, allowing all diners to fend for themselves, keep the onus from centering on one person. This regulates the dining routine and connects everyone through a daily tradition. To add to your enjoyment, assign

specific tasks, such as setting the table or cleanup, to specific family members. Getting everyone involved means that the experience will be a pleasant one for parents and children alike, rather than a fun occasion preceded or followed by drudgery.

From time to time, share memories with one another about the objects on your vintage table. Whether culled from a stellar vacation or given to you by a college roommate, these items have been given a place of honor, and sharing those associations engages others to appreciate family traditions and heirlooms. Perhaps you honor Grandma by making her favorite mashed potatoes and presenting them in a serving bowl she received as a wedding gift and later passed on to you. Or maybe the salt and pepper shakers that you take for granted because they are used every night were carved by your uncle for his big brother—known to you as Dad—many years ago. Homes that honor the kitchen and afford a place for all to meet at the table are homes that keep traditional customs alive. Creating surroundings you love perpetuates the ritual of entertaining on a daily basis.

A great kitchen is the focal point of a family gathering. Whether by setting the table or assisting with the cooking, every member can contribute to the meal.

∽ LEFT: *Durable linens* in an earthy style are pieces of art.

∽ OPPOSITE: The custom of *marketing* the *European* way, in which fresh food is purchased daily for its superior taste and healthful benefits, is a lifestyle worth emulating. This ritual will enjoyably enhance your routine.

French Marketing

French cuisine, even when as simple as a croissant with raspberry preserves, is always packed with organic style and embellished with classic pieces. The French honor what is well produced over what is fashionable. From the way they go to market to how they translate the finest ingredients into a meal, French people set their tables in a style that is a gastronomic experience, engaging all the senses.

Begin your French approach by marketing the European way. Look to see where local farmers' markets or organic specialty food stores are located in your neighborhood and become versed in the bounties such venues offer. A farmers' market, for example, is not just a place for a shopping trip but also an experience that will connect you to a community and the fine artistry of food offered at its most wholesome. An entire parking lot can become transformed into a Provençal town square, dotted with tents bursting with bright produce. Shoppers wander from stand to stand, sampling cut apples speared with toothpicks and gathering vegetables still bearing the soil of their origins into a reusable bag. You can fill a basket with an entire week's worth of food at such outings and even include such romantic additions as flowers, honey straight from the hive, and homemade organic chocolate. Such sprees also give your credit cards a break, as exchanges are typically made in cash.

Weave your fresh finds in with classic French pieces, such as glasses hugged in rattan covers, spreading knives in gingham patterns, French linens so sturdy you could pitch a tent with them, or a grouping of hemp sacks tied in bundles and coddled in a willow basket. The pieces have a timeworn feel. They possess a beauty bestowed by their primitive feel and hold up under pressure and regular use.

◠ OPPOSITE, ABOVE: Create your own trend with *handwoven baskets,* which help ease the strain on our global resources.

◠ OPPOSITE, BELOW: The French are actually *skilled minimalists* who value things that are well made, intended for constant use, and above excess.

FARMING THE FIELD

Today, with the demand for organically grown food on the rise, farmers' markets have been cropping up on urban terrain at an increasing rate. Such venues not only provide people access to fresh produce, they offer a social gathering where shoppers interact with one another and with the farmers, and where they can learn firsthand the importance of the farmers' existence—how the vitality of farms strengthens communities and promotes the availability of fresh foods in various locales.

While reaching back in time to set a table with vintage style, we create beauty by incorporating both old and new, and we find that in doing so, we've made a fresh, modern setting. These eye-pleasing, heart-filled tablescapes make our guests' senses dance, but also serving the freshest fare will make an event a truly memorable, even healthful affair. While we still may need to supplement our grocery shopping at a traditional store, farmers' markets offer us all the experience of marketing like our great-grandparents did.

Those who shop at farmers' markets also benefit from the superior taste of produce that is locally grown, such as that of arugula picked the same morning, or sun-warmed tomatoes that have traveled fewer than a hundred miles from farm to table. Visit ams.usda.gov for more information about how to find a farmers' market in your community.

↪ Get connected with your local *farmers' market*. Shopping for *farm-fresh food* is a healthy way to make your meals divine.

Get Set, Go!

Breakfast begins with a setting of hearty pewter pieces, café au lait bowls, and basic white china, all chosen for their primitive, laid-back, classic style. You can almost see the hammer impressions in the teaspoons. Eschew place mats in favor of a marble countertop, which has a nonfussy, elegant look that makes for easy cleanup and also happens to be easy on your resources. A water pitcher is the chosen vessel for a bundle of lavender pulled straight from the garden. The menu is simple and filling: brown hard-boiled eggs, fruit-filled tarts, croissants, dark- and white-grain baguettes, and coffee—lots of it and in all varieties. Clumps of brown sugar or candied sticks add ornament and taste. Such elements create a typically French ambience—easy, nourishing, and sophisticated.

The location is a humble corner chosen for its powdery, early-morning Parisian light. It's a setting that welcomes guests or provides an excuse to read the paper from cover to cover. This kind of breakfast is such a welcome way to start the day, you may linger right into lunch.

↷ ABOVE LEFT: In their individual *pewter cups,* brown *eggs* are as pretty as chess pieces, though their contribution to the table's style is no game.

↷ ABOVE RIGHT: An assortment of *fruit tarts* adds a punch of color to the subdued neutral palette.

↷ RIGHT: Breakfast the French way with a few timeless pieces. Even the baguette is artistry when paired with subtle fabrics and pewter.

↷ OPPOSITE: Very little effort goes into the *understated* sophistication of this setting. The classic appeal of this marble tabletop even renders high maintenance linens unnecessary.

COFFEE BREAK

The language used for ordering coffee has become almost scientific.
Due to coffee's many varieties, deciphering the types takes one smart bean.
Here's a glossary of the most popular coffee drinks.

AMERICAN ROAST: Medium-roasted coffee beans

CAFÉ AMERICANO: American drip coffee made using the Italian
method, with espresso and boiling water

CAFÉ LATTE: A double shot of espresso and finished with steamed milk foam

CAFÉ LATTÉ FREDDO: Shaken iced café latte

CAFÉ AU LAIT: Equal amounts brewed coffee and steamed milk

CAFÉ MACCHIATO: 1½ ounces of espresso topped with foamed milk

CAFÉ MOCHA: Espresso, chocolate syrup, and steamed milk

CAFÉ NOISETTE: Espresso with just a small amount of milk, creating a
nutty taste

CAPPUCCINO: Espresso topped with steamed and foamed milk

ESPRESSO: Robust black coffee made with densely packed coffee grounds

⌒ OPPOSITE: There are a variety of *coffee concoctions* to choose from,
but one faithful café au lait cup is all that is needed to conjure up tastes of
France.

Eating Naturally

Invite Mother Nature to your table and you will be delighted by her earthy contributions. Just look outside your window to see what nature can offer to your setting. Cachepots of herbs, clusters of pinecones, seashells, and other beach bounties are dependable contributors. Use unexpected vessels, such as mercury-glass containers, for a glamorous touch, and place starfish over a bed of sea grass.

Many vintage dish patterns and accessories celebrate nature. Pair bleached sand dollars with delicate white fiddlehead-fern-handled cups for a sweet place-setting embellishment. Fill a vintage wicker basket to overflowing with pine branches and pinecones for a rustic holiday centerpiece. Or prove that opposites attract: Dress up a table with an arrangement of curly willow branches decorated with retro sewing notions like thimbles, wooden thread spools, and Bakelite buttons hung from antique ribbons. Wholesome elements perform multiple uses and enrich a basic setting.

For drama, throw in some *metallic pieces*—such as a *mercury-glass urn*—with your natural finds.

High Tea

Perhaps there is something in those tea leaves that has made this ritual enduring. A tea service comes with dainty pieces that could easily be crushed under clumsy masculine hands. Fanciful accents and confections adorned with roses complement Granny's dishes. Pay particular attention to the small details, such as cutting the crusts from sandwiches and displaying pretty tea bags out of their paper sleeves. Guests will duly notice.

Tea varieties span the world, providing an international selection of exotic flavors, customs, and styles. It's a healthy way to start the day or to cap off the evening. From displaying loose teas in exotic jars to showing off all the fineries associated with the ritual, a tea break enlivens a table and is an easy way to entertain regularly. Of course, you can also make it a simple gathering of one. When you catch a private moment, shut down the computer and cellphone to follow through on what matters with this warm, soothing elixir in hand.

✍ LEFT AND BELOW: It doesn't matter where the occasion is held, pieces printed with *pink cabbage roses* will always call to mind an English country house.

✍ OPPOSITE: A tea need not be an extravagant affair. Sometimes it is enjoyable to preside over a *party of one*.

∽ LEFT: Every little girl should have a *pink-themed* tea party to drift away to.

∽ OPPOSITE: Playing with *Mommy's pieces* is an education in respecting finer things and makes daughters feel special.

Lower Case Tea

A children's tea is a fun way to introduce kids to the mannered world of grown-ups. They can use a miniature practice set made from crocheted coverings inserted with the kind of vessel used to serve Italian ice. Dessert silverware fits perfectly in a child's hand, while ornamental name-card holders add whimsy to the tablescape. Pretty cakes, artful chocolates, and, of course, tea with lots of sugar will be enjoyed by all. A table set with a combination of children's and adult's pieces is the perfect blend of two worlds.

Then, when the time is right, children can graduate to Mommy's dishes (second-tier ones of course), to make them feel very proper while learning to respect delicate things. These ladies-in-training will find bliss in creative play and become the kind of hostesses everyone would like to know.

TOP LEFT AND RIGHT: A true hostess doesn't hold back on the frivolous embellishments. *Ribbons and flowers* all mix together for one memorable spectacle. BOTTOM LEFT: A *pink crown* looks deliciously nonsensical atop a mountain of meringues. BOTTOM RIGHT: Simple *playing cards* are rich with color and pattern.

Theme Event

Just as children's birthday parties crib from surrounding trends—ever been to a Disney-themed party?—adults can have fun borrowing inspiration from the current zeitgeist. Whether from film, the latest fashion trend, or a classic party motif, fantastical themes can be aptly channeled into your next event.

Combine what you own with what is readily available. The inspiration can be over-the-top, such as Marie Antoinette's twenty-first birthday bash at Versailles or the Mad Hatter's tea party. A deck of cards strewn across the table directs the table arrangement. Pink pastry boxes too pretty to toss out can be used in your vignette. Cake plates, our dependable ally in creating variety and function, can display everything from sweet delicacies to baker's twine. Make room for gifts, as they add flair to the arrangement as much as sweet confections do. Flowers in mint julep cups have a fanciful style that shows Alice really has arrived in Wonderland.

Baker's twine is always a fun addition to the party. Tie it on pretty pink boxes with extra delicacies from the day as great favors.

Just Because

Holiday decorations may be collecting dust, and your birthday is months away. Days that seem to race by challenge your ability to slash through all the items on your to-do list, and tea and parlor conversation seem like a novelty from historical fiction. There is only one way to bring these niceties of yesteryear into our modern sphere: Throw a party.

Channel the hostess who trusts florists and caterers as she would her family, the fashionable lady who can work her way through a party with laser-sharp radiance and say "toodles" while balancing a jeweled headpiece on her head as if it's an everyday accessory.

Janet Rodriguez, the president and owner of Embroidery Palace Inc., a company that creates one-of-a-kind linens, may not wear a tiara to her parties, but she has certainly earned the right. At her imaginative affairs, the table becomes an

At first sight, the table is a *dazzling* spectacle of colorful pieces, flowers, and elegance. *Turquoise glassware* sets an interesting palette of pinks and touches of metallic.

exhibition piece that transports her guests, enabling them to interact within a beautiful environment. "I love to set the table," says Janet. "It's like creating a beautiful piece of art."

Evaluate your best pieces, consider everything a potential part of the composition—even if it appears excessive. This process will allow you to reconnect with great items that you may have forgotten. Perhaps you'll end up basing the theme of your next event on those gold chargers that have been occupying a spot in the back of your cabinet.

Next, edit according to your chosen focal point, using color and style as a guide. You can now graduate to the fun part of the table-setting process, where you get to decide what look you want to achieve. "Most of the time my table setting just evolves from the choices I make when deciding on what to use," Janet says. "It depends on the occasion, the company, and of course what you are serving. Is it going to be over-the-top or a casual affair?"

Janet prefers to have several options for her table. "A big butler's pantry is nice so you can get a glance at everything you own. Also, have a few sets of china, glass dishes, stemware, silverware, and plenty of place mats and chargers."

Indeed, Janet has a distinguished collection of pieces to choose from. An avid collector, she shops in a variety of venues including showrooms and on the Internet, and she seeks any opportunity to showcase these finds on her table. One of her leading collecting obsessions is opaline. Hailing from nineteenth-century France, these glass pieces have a milky appearance and come in a variety of colors. Janet's first piece was a Venetian mirror that she bought at an antiques shop in London. "I decided to use it as a reflector for the tabletop," she says. She then accumulated opaline pitchers, vases, and other special items. "My biggest find was a whole place setting for twelve," she says. "Now I am into turquoise milk glass, which works perfectly with the opaline."

"I LIKE TO USE A LOT OF *small vases* INSTEAD OF A MAIN CENTERPIECE."
—JANET RODRIGUEZ

She tucks novelty items and gorgeous tableware into every available place. Like a painting chock-full of so many details that each time you view it you come across something new, Janet always adds flourishes. "I like to have water glass that is a little different from the stemware, something colorful and whimsical. For this table, I never use a tablecloth, because the antique mirror is just too beautiful to cover up. I use a lot of candles, because they reflect the light so beautifully off the antique mirror. I like to use a lot of small vases for flowers instead of a main centerpiece. It gives the table more movement and excitement," she explains.

This is a frivolous affair, the eating-gelato-from-crystal-glasses sort. It is the grand finale, when all the players come onstage in a bright and exciting spectacle that produces thunderous applause. "Whatever the event may be," adds Janet, "I like to go all out and make my guests feel incredibly special."

In Love

There are certain no-fail ways to create a romantic ambience: candles, flowers, and a flow of libations.

In Jon Condell's Pasadena, California, home he uses his expertise as a store owner and event planner to design a table setting that inspires us with enough romantic detailing to make us expect a heroine from a paperback romance to step off the cover and into the scene. "I wanted to create a magical and romantic setting here," says Jon of this vignette, "but I wanted it to be comfortable too."

ABOVE LEFT: Flowers become *showcase* pieces when displayed beneath a *bell jar.*

ABOVE RIGHT: At the historic *Forster Mansion* in San Juan Capistrano, California, a man doesn't even have to ask his paramour the question, as the setting says it all.

OPPOSITE: You must search through the blooms and ivy to find your dinner plate, which shows that the creator of this table regards all the frills with *thoughtful* consideration.

⌒ Fine china gleams atop a refined *mahogany tabletop.* This timeless elegance creates a feeling of celebration.

Jon's intent was to make a scene. Like he has, gather your most treasured belongings to pull off this dramatic scenario. "Use your favorite pieces, and if you break something, so be it. Share them with your guests; they were meant to be used, so enjoy them," he advises.

To play off Jon's impressive collection of silver, crystal, and heirloom china, he chose bold reds and darker shades of pink—colors that pop—to balance the ornate pieces. He grouped smaller greenery and florals together, which flow off the edges to give the setting a fantastical effect. Decadent pomegranates are interspersed here and there, some cut to reveal their gemmed insides. The romantic couple is transported from a room into a magical realm where tiaras are worn and girls with braided hair get into plenty of trouble due to their questionable relationship with sorcerers.

Silver jewelry released from their chests, crystal pieces so dainty they could splinter upon being touched, and tea packaged in origami shapes bring élan to the table. It's a setting that will get her to say yes without even being asked.

TABLE SETTINGS
WITH LOVE

- Send your SIGNIFICANT OTHER a dinner invitation.
- Set the table with treasures that have MEANING to you and the ones you love.
- Fill in spaces with over-the-top EMBELLISHMENTS, such as abundant flowers, vintage cards, greenery, chocolates too pretty to eat, and exotic fruits.
- Overdo the ROMANTIC GESTURES. Impeccably dressed chocolates, champagne, and garnishes cut into the shape of a heart are all welcome.
- Select a RICH PALETTE that adds beauty to your accessories.

A More Formal Approach

A good host will find any excuse to throw a party, and for those who want to deco-
rate to the limit, creating an epic setting need not require a battalion of headset-
wearing party planners.

As the world becomes increasingly casual, there are those who will always
love an opportunity to play dress-up. Creating a luxurious table is much like
wearing your favorite cocktail attire. Consider the china, the cocktail dresses,
and all those delicious accessories of beaded clutches and jewelry as your
accent pieces.

A formal event is where the dining room gets its turn in the household's activity, with the silver polished and the good china spruced up. Use those coveted
pretties you love so. The table can emulate the formality of a state dinner or

Set out your good pieces for a *feast of glamour.*

ⓢ ABOVE: At Gracie's restaurant—in Portland, Oregon, at the *Hotel deLuxe*—a nod to vintage glamour takes hold.

ⓢ ABOVE RIGHT AND OPPOSITE: Go with silver, gold, and other *metallic pieces* for an elegant setting, but be careful not to over-bling.

ⓢ RIGHT: Pulling out your finer pieces is always a *reflective process,* as each important piece contains a story.

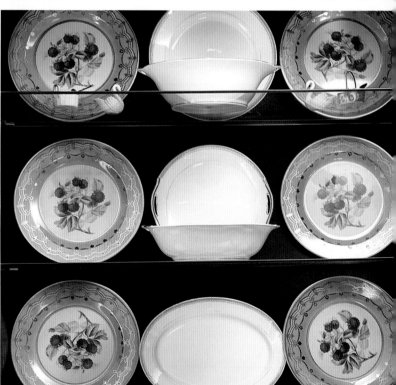

include over-the-top embellishments, such as a grandiose urn used as a center-piece and filled with frivolous trinkets like pearled shells and jeweled orna-ments. Glam worshippers will always favor sparkly metallic accessories, and today's place settings offer hundreds of enticing options. There are silvery, striped teacups a modern-day princess would use and embroidered linens gilded and chokered in jeweled napkin holders. Gold is the epitome of opulence. Place a golden starfish atop a bowl to pretend Wall Street's heyday has made a come-back. Channel the 1980s' excesses and fill your table with anything pretty and textural, such as an open book, feathers, silver accessories, and more candles than a church has at Christmastime.

ETIQUETTE BREAK
THE PROPER
TABLE SETTING

The standard place setting can start with a charger; otherwise, a dinner plate will suffice. The soup bowl is placed on top of the dinner plate. Forks are to the left, with the fork needed for the first course, typically salad, in the innermost position, closest to the plate. The knife is set to the right, with the sharp side facing in. If there is a fish course, that knife is placed next, followed by the soup spoon. The dessert spoon and cake fork are placed above the dinner plate.

On the top row, the bread plate is placed to the left, and drinking glasses are on the right. The water goblet is placed just above the knives, with the wineglasses following to the right. Napkins can be placed on top of the dinner plate or to the left of the forks.

Arranging a *proper table setting* is one of the many skills of a talented host.

✍ In Janet Solomon's *eclectic* collection, she uses more of an assortment than a set.

Hotel Hospitality

Some of the more sophisticated homes in this book possess a true vintage style that pays homage to the owners' travels. Sometimes these world travelers haven't even had to leave the hotel to develop their sophisticated palettes. Just a trip to the lobby or a drink at the hotel bar or a meal at the restaurant offers inspiration. Who hasn't stayed in a hotel without indulging in fantasies of never having to check out? Hotels understand the value of little luxuries and how to make a stay memorable. These elegant little luxuries are worth living with every day.

Mixed in with what you already own, hotel pieces are a personal way to add glamour to your table's setting. Janet Solomon's home would get high ratings in any travel magazine. Though a seasoned world traveler, her passport is mostly printed with French stamps. This Francophile returns home with luggage (Goyard, of course) filled with Parisian goodies that will inevitably get their play in her table setting. Making her way through customs, Janet will always declare France's finest chocolates and goodies from the tea-house Ladurée in packaging so pretty the boxes must be kept even after the treats are consumed. Her color palette is soft and romantic: creamy whites in simple patterns, flecks of gold here and there, and classically bold black. To create a hotel setting at home, Janet recommends doing some research. "When you travel, visit hotels for lunch or dinner. Bring back your ideas to your own table at home," she says.

Janet's table begins with her palette, usually in the form of a crisp white linen tablecloth and folded white napkins. Polished, gleaming silver adds a Grand Hotel ambience. Place settings with vintage hotel-logo dinnerware offer a unique touch.

The delicacies served are light and sophisticated, which meshes well with her collection of Astier de Villatte dishware. Astier pieces have a signature style that is both classic and modern. They come in distinctive shapes, some with ear-shaped handles and others that look like the tendrils of a pea shoot. However, with their insouciant style, they all speak French better than the French themselves. Fine chocolate set within an Astier dish bearing a big-faced flower pattern is exactly what Eloise would expect when visiting Paris.

LEFT: This collection of *hotel silver* adds ornament to your dining surroundings.

BELOW: A world-class shopper, Janet accumulates her pieces from visits to *estate sales*, flea markets, and her seasonal sojourns to *Paris*.

OPPOSITE: Dine in a *fine establishment* every night when you serve with dishware and accents sourced from a hotel.

~ LEFT: A French price card punctuates a setting by its color and provenance.

~ OPPOSITE: *Relish all the details.* That strange teapot you weren't quite sure about? Grouped with like members, it looks happily at home.

To find such unique hotel items, Janet searches hotel auctions. "When a hotel remodels, they auction off much of their hotel ware," she says. Flea markets, estate sales, hotel gift shops, and eBay are other good sources. "When shopping, keep your imagination focused on black-and-white. Tuxedo-wearing butlers with shining silver trays, serving high tea in fine bone china, and the clattering of dishes with the light dancing above you like stars; it is then you are sure to capture the perfect hotel table setting," says Janet.

In Lynn Goldfinger-Abrams's San Francisco home, she makes the most of her space-challenged rooms the way a top hotel would. Though her dining areas are small and crammed with her beloved things, they don't appear cluttered. This is because her collectibles follow the cool palette of silver, white, and sun-catching glass. There is a simple elegance to the table setting, which further romanticizes a clever flower arrangement. Even a silver dish of Hershey's miniatures appears four-star in such glam surroundings. Add in personal touches such as a bellboy cap, a letter written on hotel stationery, and patterned linens for spots of color and intrigue.

From silverware and silver table elements to guest registries, matchbooks, and ashtrays, items from hotels and swank hot spots will add beauty to your vignettes. Undoubtedly strong enough to withstand multiple uses and indulgent enough to be admired, hotel pieces are worth writing home about.

⌒ OPPOSITE LEFT, TOP AND BOTTOM: Careful thought put into the flower arrangements, such as blooms in a *container filled with grapes* or in one bordered with stalks of asparagus, makes it appear as though you have a florist on staff.
⌒ OPPOSITE RIGHT, TOP AND BOTTOM: What you serve brings accent to the table. Even an arrangement of *strawberries* puts you in a cared-for mood.

STERLING SERVICE

To collect hotel silver, Lynn Goldfinger-Abrams, proprietress
of Paris Hotel Boutique, offers the following tips:

- MIX AND MATCH All of Lynn's silver is assorted. Her shopping method is simple: She buys pieces she likes. "Most of the teapots, creamers, and pitchers in my collection are strictly decorative, not for serving purposes. If you have a piece in your collection that you want to use for serving but it is corroded on the inside, take it to a silversmith and have the interior replated. For the true collector, it's all about the provenance and design."

- ALL ABOUT DESIGN "Often the pieces with the most charm, even from unknown hotels, sell fairly quickly." Lynn says to search for side marks, crests, and logos, which add interest to the silver. "I personally have many pieces from the top hotels but also unusual pieces from unknown establishments. It's also a matter of what you think is pretty."

- GETTING PERSONAL "Some collectors strictly want hotels that have personal meaning, others go for design alone, and some just want to use pieces for serving and want the hotel quality and grade. Some people simply don't mind if there are no logos or names. They just want large hotel-grade bowls and platters for serving. So it really depends on what you like. My advice would be to collect whatever appeals to you. There are no rules."

- AGE NEED NOT MATTER "Age should not be a factor in collecting hotel silver. If the piece is well made and is by an old manufacturer such as Gorham or Reed & Barton, it's highly collectible. Avoid limiting a collection to certain time periods or the geographic location of the hotel. If you were ever to sell the collection, it would be a lot more interesting to another collector to have pieces from a variety of hotels, including ones in San Francisco and New York. The detail and workmanship is great, and they don't make things like this anymore."

- IN ALL LIKELIHOOD "Go for what you like and what strikes a chord. Pieces with raised crests, interesting shapes, and monograms are always good choices."

∽ TOP LEFT AND RIGHT: Silver from noted hotels is highly collectible;
however, interesting pieces that are *unmarked* or are from lesser establishments will
always hold *value*. ∽ BOTTOM LEFT: It is easily evident that Lynn enjoys
collecting hotel pieces for her settings, where she arranges her silver with *whimsy*
and style. ∽ BOTTOM RIGHT: Collect what you like, even if it is unusable.
Pieces can be repaired, or they hold their own based on their *decorative* appeal.

SET THE SETTING

Hosting an event is more than just entertaining a group of friends, it's about creating an environment. To become an entertainer, follow this personal exploration to help you find your own style. You may find that you prefer large family gatherings or intimate one-on-one dinners. Whatever your preference, look for ways to help you perfect your skills.

1. FIND INSPIRATION for your table in places other than your cupboard. Magazines, films, and artwork can lead you to a theme. You may love the colorful images found in fairy tales and Elizabethan novels, for example. Film adaptations of classic stories can transport you to another time, adding details you may want to use, such as fine china at a picnic or cupcakes with sparklers poked into the middle. The result is truly cinematic.

2. SOCIALIZE. Accept those invitations no matter how filled your agenda may be. Novel ideas can be found at the fortieth wedding anniversary held for your parents' best friends. Give your sister a needed break and accompany your nieces to a birthday party, which may feature bubbles and pink fairy lights that become the highlights at your next affair.

3. Do some ONLINE RESEARCH and hit the party sites and events sites. You may stumble upon the most adorable Chinese lanterns and paper umbrellas with which to compose a theme around.

4. TRAVEL AND DINE OUT. Not only will time away from home rejuvenate you, but you'll also learn how fine establishments understand the importance of memorable details to make their guests feel welcome. Bring your diary along with you to your next visit, and jot away.

3

The

SEASONS

Entertaining Through the Year

Our lives follow the *patterns* of the seasons. We wear light jackets with a rubbery veneer to protect us in the rainy transition between spring and summer, and sweaters and thick socks in winter. We have *seasonal tastes;* watermelon just doesn't have the same appeal when our feet are defrosting from a cold day outside. We are as *predictable* as geese flying south for the winter. When the first hint of *frost* starts the morning, our senses react. We follow what is happening outdoors, and the table makes one of the many *transformations* that take place four times a year. Weather patterns shape the environment and thereby the *landscape* of our table.

*ABOVE LEFT: Christmas tree ornaments need not remain on the tree. Stacked together they provide a festive centerpiece.

*ABOVE RIGHT: Gourds of all varieties line the stairs to this harvest event, creating an enchanting autumn environment.

*OPPOSITE: Vintage elements celebrating the Fourth of July will set a patriotic-themed table.

Like little prizes found in a cereal box, holidays are special treats that are enclosed among the calendar's more humdrum days. We put a lot of emphasis on these celebratory days, as they mean mandatory entertaining. Each season affords us the opportunity to test a new style, and the experience we've accrued over the course of the previous year means we bring something new to the table each time we entertain.

⌒○ RIGHT AND OPPO-
SITE, TOP ROW: For more
formal affairs, combine your best
pieces with colorful accents that
carry the notes of the season.

⌒○ OPPOSITE, BOTTOM
ROW: Select accessories that
parlay the theme of the setting
and relate to what is happening
outdoors.

⌒ SPRING ⌒

Like the fresh start that's offered by a winter thaw, the year according to the table
also begins with spring. After peeling off all those restricting layers or perhaps
seeing the world in Technicolor again, you may suddenly find that you have a
hankering for cabbage rose patterns and all the flowery accents, Easter egg colors,
and soft textures that complement them.

Spring fosters a lighter mood that will be revealed on the table. It can be a
simple, elegant affair where a few star pieces glimmer under sunnier light. Or you
might surrender to spring's seduction and forgo the ironed napkins for more
informal linens. They do say that wrinkles add character.

Draw table-setting ideas from the whimsy of paper umbrellas or the sherbet
tones of melon balls. Dishes, arbitrarily set here and there, can also follow this carefree pattern. Such an approach keeps your mood and the setting casual and fun.

❧ RIGHT: The table is set with a mix of new and vintage pieces. Different *patterns* and periods unite through shared colors and texture.

❧ OPPOSITE, LEFT: Purple *lilacs* complement this unique tea pitcher.

❧ OPPOSITE, RIGHT: Annette Tatum combines newer finds with pieces that have been passed down and relate through color and style, for a seamlessly personalized look.

En Plein Air

After spending so much time indoors that bare legs prickle at the slightest gust of wind, our first impulse in spring is to be outside whenever possible. Dining en plein air, French for "in the open air," is one of spring's most anticipated pleasures and calls for a lively atmosphere. Influenced by the season's fresh bounties and colors, the food we serve suggests itself. Flowers are so abundant you can forgo florists for what's available in your own garden.

At designer Annette Tatum's home in Santa Monica, California, inspired dining outdoors is a regular happening. Known for her romantic bedtime collection, House Inc., Annette is also a gifted entertainer, and, blessed with Southern California temperatures, she hosts a great deal of dining outside, even if spring hasn't yet arrived in other regions. Her terrace is separated from the kitchen and main room by a wall of glass doors. The floors are a mosaic blanket of tiles that appears to have been transported from the courtyard of a Moroccan palace. As a designer known to agonize over just the right tone to shape her next lingerie line, she bestows equally meticulous attention on the hues chosen for her tabletop. In fact,

she gave the bakery that created the cake for a party an assortment of Pantone chips to ensure that the dessert would complement her fresh lilacs and dinnerware. Her mix of heirlooms, antique finds, and a joyful china set from Anthropologie is like the floral luxuries she creates, stocked with soft, feminine colors and patterns that all come together in an elegant crescendo.

While we tend to regard an outdoor dining setting as casual, Annette finds that it is just as simple to go glam. Her signature setting uses more formal indoor elements, such as silverware, china, and furnishings, for a richer look. "Dining outside is not always about a picnic," says Annette. "We should all bring indoor things out more often. I love the idea of bringing formal furniture out." Some of the unexpected accents include chandeliers, curtains, old books, and framed oil paintings. "Full-length mirrors or outdoor urns are great ways to adorn an outdoor space as well. I have pulled out my Louis XV gilded chairs and side tables. Once, we pulled the couches onto the grass to create a comfy lounge space."

Guests enjoy the comfort and elegance of such indoor attractions in the fresh air of an outdoor setting. "Outside, unbound by walls, you are able to have a more inviting experience," says Annette.

ABOVE: A setting is warmed by *spring light,* which illuminates treasured pieces and spots of lilies of the valley collected from outside.

RIGHT: Various accessories, such as *vintage perfume bottles,* complete the theme.

TOILET WATER
(EAU DE TOILETTE)
MUGUET
des Bois
COTY
MONTREAL · PARIS
CONTENTS
2 FL. OZS.

Valley of the Dolls

Lilies of the valley begin their annual dance, popping from the defrosted earth, a sign of the new season. They entice with their sweet scent and their sinewy stems capped with fluted hats. Throw a party in honor of this auspicious signal, and call upon your best china and keepsake pieces, which will be humbled in a less formal location than your dining room.

At Donald Kirkby's home in Sechelt, British Columbia, Canada, a guest- house becomes the setting for an intimate gathering. Donald transformed the location with furnishings pulled from more stately parts of the house to give this space a special treatment. "This setting was created with a spring luncheon in mind," says Donald. "Nothing too elaborate, but still fancy, very traditional yet freshened up by the crispness of the spring greens and the sharp whites."

Set alongside our featured flower, such pieces glamorize these cheerful har- bingers of spring. "The elements [china, flatware, linens] are brought out of the closet to create a shining tablescape. The intensity of the high spring sun is echoed in the gold rims of the water glasses," he says.

For the hostess with the Mostest

She taught you to put your napkin on your lap and that saying "please" and "thank you" was your contribution to creating a more thoughtful world. At times she could be demanding, and it was frustrating that she always got to set the rules, but then she'd surprise you by granting your request to have chocolate for Saturday breakfast. For all of this, she gets only one day, and for this reason, we must make it memorable.

On Mother's Day eschew an uninspired brunch or luncheon and instead offer tiny pastries so delicate that they disintegrate upon hitting your tongue. Throw a party in her honor and invite all your other favorite mother-and-daughter pairs. As fabulous and fun as Mom's coconut cream pie, the theme calls for guests to wear their favorite apron and bring one baked good. Or, for those whose stoves serve as a storage space for extra bottles of wine, enlist a favorite bakery for pretty goodies without the prep work.

↪ Playing with the retro idea, *pies* and artifacts from the days of drive-ins and soda fountains give this gathering *doo-wop energy*.

There are as many varieties of pies and aprons as there are moms, guaranteeing a fete that is colorful, imaginative, warm to the tummy, delicious, and a bit retro. Rich in history, aprons are more than pieces of stringed cloth worn to protect the clothes beneath. Full, or bib, aprons protect the entire front of your clothes from below the neck to below the knees; half, or waist, aprons cover you from the waist to just above the knees. Cobbler's aprons are pulled over the head and then are tied with string closures on each side; they have many pockets and provide protection from the neck to just past the waist. Whether wearing festive hostess aprons—in any style, but always made with fine fabrics to wear over cocktail attire—or displaying them in vignettes, these moms understand the value in a pretty apron with vintage appeal.

Punchy visual accents, starting-my-diet-tomorrow pies, and guests throwing out one-liners that will make Mae West seem prim equal a boisterous fete that will make Mom proud. Pink-labeled wine bottles purchased from a boutique wine vendor and vintage cookbooks and kitchen accessories add to the look, but the real scene stealers are the aprons, especially if you're someone who enjoys an *I Love Lucy* marathon on TV Land. Cynthia Waddell, the designer of Heavenly Hostess, is of the school that believes deviled eggs are haute cuisine, and she has

channeled such ideals into her stylings. She has brought back the glam of the fifties and sixties in her accessories, which range from vintage prints dramatized by her use of bustier patterns to saucy skirts that would look right at home on a socialite at a high-profile fund-raiser to save an ailing monument. "Aprons, to me, are both retro and modern, as they are timelessly symbolic of serving those we love," says Cynthia. "Aprons are donned when serving a home-cooked meal, while hosting Mother's Day. While our personal style changes through the years, one's love of entertaining and desire to look fabulous doing it remains constant."

The setting follows the giddy pattern of one of Cynthia's aprons. If you have a kitchen that is conducive to hosting more guests, plot your party there. Add festive touches, like swap-meet finds you bought without being certain what they were originally intended for. Pages from your mother's cookbook delight with their overt kitschiness, and you may even stumble across a recipe for a pie that will be in such demand it will be sliced into tenths.

Such attention to detail will make Mom beam with pride; this is a party that will build memories. "Wearing a beautiful apron during a Mother's Day celebration lets Mom know she is loved, that she is in for a special day, and that someone else will be doing the dishes!" says Cynthia. Guests dressed in bona fide cocktail attire keep the mood festive, where the host feels she is at her most fabulous, and everyone is in for a good time.

Forget quick-fix floral deliveries in favor of celebrating Mom with elements from the *past and present*, which reflect the meaning behind the holiday.

ABOVE RIGHT: New or old? The past and present come together in a vintage-inspired *apron*, proof that great style isn't a trend.

↶ RIGHT: An entire meal can center on one *luscious watermelon*. Against its electric pinkness, neutral dishes take on a supporting role.

↶ OPPOSITE: Ask your child for permission to use his or her *red wagon,* an adorable and efficient means of transporting your outdoor tabletop needs and of keeping the *spirit of childhood* alive for everyone.

↶ SUMMER ↶

Warmer temperatures beckon us to the outdoors. If you happen to be inside instead, taking the outdoors inside is par for the course. Fresh colors are seen in the available fruits of summer and in gardens that are always putting on a show. With its explosive red, white, and blue, our nation's birthday can't get any louder. All of these summertime elements can translate to a table setting.

Summer may be the most nostalgic time of the year, perhaps because it tends to evoke childhood and its innocence. Who doesn't miss the kind of days when you assumed an alias and, with your trusted dog Scout, explored the neighborhood creek as if it were enemy terrain, taking Popsicle breaks in between missions? Swimming, beach activities, and forts built from sand fill these sunny days. Dining is dictated by this magical mood, whereby the table's location and its display have an enchanted quality. More than just a place to plop the Weber grill, your backyard and garden become captivating territory, the site of gatherings

OPPOSITE: Even a setting arranged inside contains notes of what's happening outside, as the colors, *fresh fruits,* and flowers bring *organic beauty* to the table.

ABOVE LEFT: July Fourth is not just our nation's birthday but also a celebration of summer and its *nostalgic carefree* approach. Its colors and accents add whimsy to the setting.

RIGHT: An enchanting *veranda* tucked away from the formality of the main house is an ideal canvas for a future gathering.

that will build memories. You might create a simple table surrounded by mysteri‑ ous trees or an elegant table with chandeliers, nestled within a soft sheath of curtains. The table can have stacks of plates and napkins randomly interspersed or follow the formal precision of an elegant setting. Use summer's longer days to entertain on all levels to make the season last.

Summer encourages a simple way of life, one that celebrates the treasured traditions of a more innocent time, a time that feels as if it will never end—if only because you don't want it to!

Dishing on Summer

If you want your summer romance to last, choose dishware that is classic and that makes you smile. It should have enduring qualities, whether it is handcrafted or the dishes you used when you were a child. If these pieces made it through your terrible twos, they should withstand another generation of use. These are the dishes you want to see every day of the year, just like a loved one.

As with all seasonal changes, your taste will be dictated by what's happening outside. Lighter fare replaces hearty comfort food, and the freezer needs to be adjusted to make room for more flavors of ice cream. For loose and easy affairs, forgo your everyday dishes for plastic plates that can double as Frisbees. Supplement the setting with things you already own to create a personalized table with modern vintage style, which is always practical.

LEFT: Textural accents, such as linens and *wicker chairs,* create a warm and inviting environment. OPPOSITE, TOP LEFT: *Ice-cream glasses* in Jolly Rancher tones add a spot of seasonal color to an otherwise neutral palette.
OPPOSITE, TOP RIGHT: These dishes by Irish designer *Nicholas Mosse* are hand-thrown and sponge-painted, which is the essence of one-of-a-kind style. OPPOSITE, BOTTOM: A table in bright hues and soft accents contributes to the look of a new season.

JICKIE TORRES
PROVIDES A BRIEF HISTORY OF
THE BIRTH OF A RETRO CLASSIC

Melamine, a laminate-and-plastic composite material closely associated with summer patio ware, has a history that goes farther back than the kiddie sets and cafeteria trays we remember from grade school. In fact, it was invented by a German scientist in the 1830s and became prized for its lightweight durability and easy moldability, which allowed it to retain its shape after curing. A half century later, the British had refined its use for consumer products in the home by developing what they called Beetleware, the first official plastic plates, marketed for use in picnics and for travel. In 1937 an Ohio company began to successfully mass-produce melamine dinnerware, which they called Melmac. Unlike Beetleware, Melmac stood up to repeated washings. The American public had to wait its turn, however, as melamine was, in a sense, commandeered by the United States military for use on navy ships during World War II. However, in the 1950s, as the boys in blue came back to shore, they brought their melamine with them, popularizing the material for casual dining. Melamine remained trendy up until the 1970s, when Tupperware became the new wonder material to sweep the American household.

Today, melamine is a summer staple. Its heat resistance and near indestructibility make it ideal for around the pool and barbecue. Typically available in bright, fun colors, melamine also appeals to boutique designers because of its easily printable nature. Dinnerware in this material is now offered in sophisticated artsy designs and elegant motifs. Styles range from polka dots to a plastic version of the china set *Pride and Prejudice* heroine Elizabeth Bennet would have coveted.

When collecting original Melmac from the fifties and sixties, look for pieces created by Russel Wright, Branchell, and American Cyanamid, who were among the pioneers in the mass production of melamine. Also sold as sets under the labels "Flair," "Fortiflex," and "Color-Flyte," these vintage pieces will be a charming addition to the contemporary collection in your summer stockpile.

↶ RIGHT: This setting captures the *romantic* look of summer with a garden that has separate spaces carved out for the grown-ups and kids.

↶ OPPOSITE, TOP LEFT: Too-pretty-to-eat pastries and delicate pieces are the basis of this gathering that celebrates the notion of fairies and spirits.

↶ OPPOSITE, TOP RIGHT: Pink and green *Depression glass* works well with vintage linens. Add some mother-of-pearl cutlery, which is like jewelry for the table.

↶ OPPOSITE, BOTTOM: For entertainer Diane Sedo, the fairy theme came naturally, as she collects anything related to these winged creatures.

Winged Victory

"Check the forecast for a bright day, which is the best time to catch fairies"—such is the wording on the invitations sent for a party that would have made Walt Disney smile. The elements needed for this fairy-themed fete are an enchanting garden and a group of imaginative ladies (or ladies-in-training) who all have the desire to put the world on pause and escape into the magical realm of make-believe.

Here, there is no mention of news items, the price of oil, or colds you cannot shake—such chatter scares off fairies. Instead, all attention should be directed to sampling sweets that are nearly too pretty to eat. Keep the kettle boiling for many tea runs, and have delicate cups at the ready.

A Glad
Greeting

May each day be as bright
And glad as you desire!
And its joys attain the height
To which your hopes aspire

The
Toadfla
Fairy.

Illustrated flower-
fairy books dating to
the 1920s are kept out
to be enjoyed by guests
and read to the little
ones. Cosette, the "fairy
of honor," is a natural
hostess who fits into her
wings with great style.

Though fit for Cinderella before her carriage turned back into a pumpkin, this gathering doesn't require any magic wands to create. Diane Sedo, creator of Sentimental Celebrations, is the author of this themed party, which she designed with the aim of keeping fuss and prep work to a minimum. She envisioned a celebration of winged creatures: Diane has always had a fascination with fairies and collects related pieces such as vintage dishware adorned with dragonflies, cards, and, most notably, Margaret Tarrant and Cicely Mary Barker's wonderfully illustrated books of flower fairies that date to the 1920s.

A fairy party is an ideal setting for the vintage table, with its timeless theme and its ability to turn us all into little girls again. "Many cultures have stories about fairies or sprites. A lot of these stories are closely intertwined with the natural world," says Diane. "As children, we read or listened to these stories, and they transported us to a different, imaginary realm that appealed to our sense of wonder."

Diane chose the romantic cottage garden of her friend Jeri Cunningham as the venue for this event. "I wanted it to look as though it was a room in my home, an extension of my living space," Jeri says. Thus, she carved out outdoor rooms within her backyard, adding an iron gazebo and outfitting a space beneath a one-hundred-year-old fruit tree with an old iron bed dressed with vintage pillows. A setup like this is ideal for separating the adults from the children while keeping everyone in view of one another.

Diane decorated with such romantic embellishments as paper lanterns, vintage dinner pieces, and rolls of ribbon, which are draped loosely here and there to create an airy look. "Anything soft will do, such as mixing pastels in with your vintage items," she says.

Such attention to detail makes this affair worthy of immortal guests. Diane rolls napkins into roses and makes her delicacies in the shapes of fairy effects such as leaves, fruits, and butterflies. Crown cookies are printed with guests'

⌒ LEFT: These little *floral-topped tarts* look magically real in a fantasy setting.

⌒ OPPOSITE, RIGHT: *Dragonfly cookies* are the number one choice for fairy diets. Diane outlined the cookie with a soft green shade of royal icing and let it dry for an hour. She piped the head and detail, worked down the body with *lavender icing*, and created a lace effect on the wing with white icing.

names, to be used as place cards. A pink cake adorned with dragonfly cookies is given the cutesy name "Flight of Fancy Fairy Cake." Fairy nectar (water made pink with a touch of red food coloring) is left out in hopes of attracting fairies; with this, all guests become little girls.

Hostesses with the most challenging agendas can purchase the menu items at any supermarket, and the favors are easy to find or improvise. The floral cupcakes here, for instance, are from a supermarket. Diane scraped off the frosting and used tube icing to form small petals and leaves with an applicator that can be bought at a crafts store such as Michael's.

Children and the Vintage Table

Some of the younger guests are given wings for the party, which makes them feel like they've been put under the most pleasant of spells. Despite the frivolity of the costuming and purple-frosted confections, the children learn the value of proper manners and to respect fine pieces. It is okay to introduce kids to your china so they can learn to appreciate and care for such treasures at an early age. Says Diane, "Children learn to take care of nice things by being allowed to *be* around nice things. I wouldn't put out irreplaceable family heirlooms for an event where a lot of very young children were in attendance, but there is nothing wrong with using good china and nice tablecloths when children are present." In fact, children love to try new things, so you can make a little game out of teaching them how to do a proper place setting. Another treat is to offer them silk or fresh flowers (thorns removed, please) and small jars and ribbons to make their own centerpieces.

There's always the risk that a minor disaster along the lines of a broken teacup may happen, and it may lead children to ask the inevitable question of why a bit of fairy dust can't fix it. Being pulled into the land of reality by such a mishap is probably its worst consequence and, fortunately, one that also teaches children an important lesson. Sometimes treasures break, but they will always be remembered. "Sites like eBay can help us locate replacement items without too much difficulty," adds Diane. "At events with children, one fun way to include nice things is to use mismatched cups, saucers, and plates in similar colors at the table. If any items are accidentally broken, no one will be able to tell!"

The afternoon was filled with songs and, naturally, the reading of fairy tales. "Thoughtfulness, love, and creativity all go into creating a table setting for a timeless gathering," says Diane.

ADIES
and gay
most
ing day,
I hear them
say

The other a Lily
speaks of Heaven above.

*Diane Sedo Recommends
the Following
Fairy-Approved Accents
for Your Party*

- An interesting and unexpected *centerpiece* using unique collectibles or unusual *flowers.*
- Personal touches such as using *place cards* or themes relating to the personal interests of the guests or the guest of honor.
- Careful use of color and the *blending of patterns* throughout the table-setting design to create a harmonious look.
- Attention to detail and providing guests with *interactive* elements such as costumes or books, for a memorable day.

ABOVE: Rather than setting one centerpiece, a variety of unique items are sprinkled over the table. A vintage card inserted in a flower frog unites the theme.

OPPOSITE, LEFT: Guests are overwhelmed by the opportunity to eat such pretty confections.

SMALL
ACHIEVEMENTS

The best resource for the modern vintage table may be the most innocent one—
kids! Who is more in tune with what is going on today than the next generation?
Not only will your table have a fresh and young style, it will foster these future
designers' talents and will add fun to the process. Here are a few steps to get the
young ones involved:

- Take your children and young friends along with you on your SHOPPING
  EXPEDITIONS. So many designers and style arbiters I have spoken with
  were themselves afforded such EXCURSIONS at a young age. This trains
  a child's eye while educating him or her in the process of making an
  acquisition.

- Ask for their OPINIONS. Why do they like a particular piece? What
  inspires them? Where have they seen a table setting that they are drawn to?
  These are the current TRENDSETTERS, so tap into their young ideas.

- Let them HELP you pick pieces that will be used for the table. Arranging the pieces with kids is a perfect opportunity to educate them in
  MANNERS AND ETIQUETTE, which will benefit your future
  gatherings.

ABOVE LEFT: With no shortage of *collectibles* to choose from, it's no wonder that Adrienne Caldwell incorporates her vintage finds onto the table. RIGHT: Pieces do not always have to be used for their intended purpose; instead, infuse every gathering with the new and *unexpected*. OPPOSITE: Adrienne's table setting relates to her home's motto, *"Live with what you love."*

Seconds, Please

Adrienne Caldwell shares her modest home with her husband, Ron; two cats; and about a zillion collectibles. She and Ron find pleasure in living among things with a past. From vintage Pez dispensers to tea towels once used to dry milk shake glasses, vintage keepsakes find their way onto her tabletop.

With summer's warmer temperatures, meals are always outdoors—Adrienne and Ron's favorite place to dine. "I think everything looks and tastes better when served outside," says Adrienne. The season is perfect for Adrienne's childlike aesthetic; she offers ice-cream cones, frozen candy bars, and the kind of sandwiches they'd serve at a southern Florida bathing club called the Pink Flamingo.

Adrienne's table could be a cure for seeing the glass half-empty, with its bright, cheerful display. She also has fun with accents, using children's sand buckets as serving dishes and rolling wide ribbon down the center of a tablecloth for color and contrast at minimal expense.

It comes as no surprise that Adrienne's favorite color is red, which composes most of her themes, right down to the strawberry jam—Ron's favorite—she serves for a morning gathering. Always resourceful, Adrienne uses the empty jam jars to hold small bouquets of flowers. "I also love to use cocktail shakers and lunch box Thermoses for flowers as well as old metal coffee pots. I serve rolls in an old vintage strainer lined with a colorful napkin, and a colander also works well."

With so many accents to choose from, Adrienne must employ some method to her decorating. Ron calls it "structured chaos." Directed by color, function, and pattern, the table is a friendly combination of red gingham, rose prints, and polka dots. There is always a mix of old and new, where chirpy plastic plates that would work nicely at a country square dance blend with her colorful finds and

~ Red is the trusted *unifier* when there is an overwhelming display to choose from, part of Adrienne's *"structured chaos"* method.

basic glass dishware. "I try to use as many collectibles as possible, to create a warm and inviting table. Old creamers and sugar bowls are great with tea lights in them; old salt and pepper shakers add a fun, whimsical touch. Saucers without the matching cups are always easy to find in many seasonal colors and patterns. I use banana-split dishes as well as vintage soda glasses and sherbet dishes for pickles, olives, celery, mayo, etc. I mix and match dishes, solids, checks, and flowers and milk-glass pieces for a fresh look," she enumerates.

Since summer moves at a slower pace, retro pieces fall perfectly into this mode. They remind us of days when we anticipated the sound of the Good Humor truck's bell, soda pop from the bottle, and Radio Flyer wagons. Weaving these hallmarks from the past into your present-day style keeps them fresh.

SUMMER STAGE

Romantic Homes contributing editor Hillary Black is a natural when
it comes to outdoor entertaining. Hillary offers her tips on how to create
a memorable statement when entertaining:

Though it looks very top-drawer, it is easy to put your designer imprint on such a setting with fresh elements like fruits and flowers. Most of us crave the timeless experience of dining al fresco. Sharing such a meal with family and friends leaves your senses dazzled by nature and the aromatic combination of fresh food and the outdoors. In the garden, make a few inviting spots that encourage peaceful lingering for guests to enjoy before or after dining. Bowls of colorful fruits, a pitcher of cool lemonade, sparkling juice or tea, and pretty stemmed glasses should be available for casual enjoyment. Cloth napkins are a rich touch, as are plenty of pillows. A few small blankets or quilts should be at the ready in anticipation of a cool evening.

Luxury and elegance abound, along with the use of color and texture, to create an inviting ambience. For example, bright orange kumquats propped against turquoise tableware creates high drama whether in sunshine or by candlelight. Fresh hydrangeas, simply arranged, add a cool blue to soothe the senses when set at eye level to those seated at the table. Nearby, low garden walls offer additional seating, which is softened with luxurious cushions tossed outside for the day. Fabrics draped on a pergola add flair while creating a cozy gathering place. Take some tips from the pros and spice up your next al fresco dining experience with sophistication and glamour. Your guests will appreciate the lavish, royal treatment and are sure to remember your hospitality and impeccable design sense.

CLOCKWISE FROM TOP LEFT: Shop according to your affair. Serving handsomely packaged lemonade adds a welcoming detail. • Grouping a variety of items delights the eye. Use what you have, along with items reflecting the season. • A mix of styles and eras looks elegant when color pulls everything together. Here, punches of *turquoise* set off lime-green accents against a neutral palette of brown, tan, and pewter.

～ FALL ～

Fall has a rich, nutty texture, from its harvest bounties to Halloween, featuring bionic-sized pumpkins in fiery colors. Autumn is also when we begin to spend more time indoors. Food becomes heartier, cooking may take a whole day when you're making soups or baking apple pies, and the heavy dishes are brought out for serving such comfort food. Now is the time to reunite yourself with those finer pieces that were given the summer off, to spruce up your dining room and pull open the cupboard doors for your first gathering of the season.

Emulate the colors of a maple tree as it puts on its final show before its leaves fall. Native American artifacts, an interesting tray with a butterfly in flight, mounted stag horns, and stacks of Pendleton blankets bring warm texture and vivid tones to the setting. Embellish warm cider and tea with sticks of cinnamon, used to swirl your drinks to the movement of fall. Tabletop props such as pinecones, leaves, and feathers can be found outdoors as well. Bell jars showcasing apple tarts as if they were baubles in a jewelry store pique a guest's anticipation.

Harvest Gathering

If it's the kind of day when lawns become mini football fields and all that's needed is a heavy sweater, it's also a day to take advantage of what may be your last opportunity to dine outdoors. Taking a cue from harvest days, when farmers build an appetite from gathering as much from the earth as possible, natural bounties are colorful, delicious additions to the table.

A basic picnic table can be transformed into a theatrical autumnal display. Overdo it with as many pumpkins as you can, in all colors and sizes, which lends a more genuine, freshly-picked-from-the-patch feel. Amber goblets turned over become eye-catching pieces that reflect the fall light.

◌ OPPOSITE, LEFT: A *rustic* cabin porch sets the tone for this *fall gathering*. The chosen colors play off the surroundings.

◌ OPPOSITE, RIGHT: Each place setting is gifted with an *acorn truffle* that would be the envy of nearby squirrels.

◌ ABOVE LEFT: A *pear* serves as a one-of-a-kind place card holder, befitting the season.

◌ ABOVE RIGHT: Details unify the harvest theme.

In the same way that you dress for autumn temperatures, use layers on your tabletop. You can start with a basic cloth in a tone that anchors the tablescape and then add blankets or rich, heavy fabrics with paisley prints. Tied like a little boy's sack dangling from a stick, vintage burlap tea cloths have their own appeal when bone-handled utensils are tucked within. A simple pear becomes a place card holder, with guests' names written on leaves and tied with a ribbon.

A WHITER APPROACH

For a more sophisticated take on fall's palette, choose black and white (they also make for a nice gothic take on Halloween). A display of black-and-white transferware is elegant yet mildly spooky when a grinning skeleton makes a surprise appearance. Your white china set and silver pieces get a seasonal touch, and a cake plate trimmed with a silver pinecone border and white pumpkins distinguishes the tablescape. Ornament the table with folk pieces, Halloween crackers, and hand-painted eggs that show personal style.

∿BOTTOM LEFT: Black and white *transferware* is used to create a *gothic scene* that has a modern feel owing to its untraditional color. ∿OPPOSITE: An elegant approach to this earthy season is to use *white china* set off with flourishes from outdoor elements.

Thanksgiving Romance

Loosen the rules for your traditional Thanksgiving dinner with thoughtful touches. Leave the warty gourds and marshmallow side dishes on the kiddie table. When it comes to creating a Thanksgiving celebration with romance, throw some unexpected details into your holiday preparation. At the Ramos House Café in San Juan Capistrano, California, owner John Humphreys creates a memorable setting that has vintage appeal.

It certainly helps that John's restaurant and home are situated in a classic bungalow, right in the center of a historic neighborhood. The charming environs is complete with the rumbles of passing trains and an old wagon on the property, which is a recurring focal point for many en plein air backdrops.

> "PREPARING A THANKSGIVING *fete* DOES NOT HAVE TO BECOME A DAUNTING TASK."

"I try to work with the elements that already exist and complement them," John says. "For example, my home is turn-of-the-century old board and batten, and I couldn't change that even if I wanted to."

Decorative yet functional accents play off this formidable foundation, such as jam jars used as drinking glasses and heavy pewter utensils. John also looks to burlap, gas lanterns, and copper wine buckets to build on the nostalgic feel. His antique gramophone adds to the novelty, and somehow the music seems to sound better when crooned from that witch's hat of a speaker.

"Not that gramophones existed in 1621, but I usually crank mine up and spin some old seventy-eights. That seems to get everyone feeling nostalgic," John says. The music keeps to the beat of the affair, and John assures a playlist that elevates moods. "I play Johnny Cash or the blues because classical just wouldn't work," he adds.

A traditional menu is always appreciated—you wouldn't want to disappoint Uncle Willard by depriving him of his annual three pieces of pumpkin pie. Wine and refreshing cocktails should be offered to keep family moments silly and

OPPOSITE, LEFT: A bright mix of *exotic blooms* offers a lively contrast with the rural wood siding of the patio walls. Such unexpected elements add visual punch and create dynamic vignettes.

OPPOSITE, RIGHT: Look for *farmhouse-style* components for table settings, such as using jam jars as vases.

PRECEDING PAGE: A fall setting of harvest *pies* is crowned by an ethereal arrangement of *hydrangeas* and feathers.

loose. Large jars of dried cranberries and nuts add beauty while also providing satisfying nibbles until the main course arrives. Classic pies and the featured turkey remind guests of the meaning of this day.

The table setting is softened with a color palette that's more soothing than the expected autumnal browns and reds. "We set up a few stations to keep the occasion loose and carefree," John says. One table has an earthy tablecloth printed with sprigs of lavender and fresh bundles of the herb splashed here and there, along with an arrangement of feathers and flowers, to add beauty and a palatable scent. On another table is a basic piece of fabric that has been ironed on its underside to create a runner. The delicate pattern of pale peach, green, and purple florals is the scheme that Amanda Heer of Fantasy Floral Designs used to create the star centerpiece.

When setting an arrangement that would make the Impressionists gush in delight, Amanda keeps it simple yet provocative. "I began with a candlescape of assorted shapes, clustered together, then added fruits and loose flower heads. Choose available flowers in unexpected colors such as deep pinks, soft peaches, light apricots, and antique ivory," says Amanda. Mini vegetables in interesting colors, which can be found in most markets, add to the festive appeal. Amanda used her own whitewashed urn and recommends working with your favorite container. Also consider such simple arrangements as herbs planted in a vintage pot.

Preparing a Thanksgiving fete does not have to become a daunting task. Find inspiration in the things you already own, share these bounties with guests, and add something inspiring to the mix. Overall, you will be the host of a festive gathering that offers second—and third and fourth—helpings of pleasure.

✎ OPPOSITE: The shimmer of goblets march below festive details that play on winter's splendor.

✎ LEFT: A bowl of silver pinecones is an eye-catching and unexpected centerpiece.

✎ WINTER ✎

In creating the winter table, draw inspiration from fables about clever little creatures who have the ability to turn the most banal object into something magical. Since not all of us hail from places called Anandor, where flowing rivers are the color of night stars, we must substitute mysticism for imagination. The process is a form of time travel, where you consider your most memorable holidays, evaluate all your pieces, no matter how plain, and envision how they can be dramatized.

Winter is rich with textual imagery. Perhaps from all the time we spend escaping uncompromising weather and talking about Saint Nick's chimney-diving and turbo-charged sleigh, we seem to have a looser grasp on reality when it comes to winter entertaining. Decorations can be over-the-top. Throw in superfluous things that shimmer. Take a few pages from those fabled Christmas stories and transfer them onto your table.

Holiday Fete

Standard holiday-motif table settings are about as ho-hum as Santa's red hat. Instead, find interest in a gathering that could be held within an enchanted forest sans the frigid temperatures. Have all your most glistening objects report to duty, such as mercury-glass ornaments, glass icicles, and enough fantastical elements to make an elf feel underutilized. An imperfect Christmas tree looms over the setting, its scented branches dangling like hands seductively luring a lover. Include pastries with the intri-cate detailing of an Icelandic sweater, pome-granates cracked open so you can peek at their jeweled insides, and a stack of willing gingerbread men waiting to be seized upon for the sake of a happy gathering. If Charles Dickens were snatched from his environs and dropped into this fete, he'd feel that only his attire was out of place.

At the McCharles House in Old Tustin, California, Audrey and Vivian Heredia love the holidays so much that they keep their decorations up through February 2 to commemorate Candlemas Day, a Christian festival of lights that marks the midpoint of winter, halfway to the spring equinox. "Decorating for the holidays starts with a

CLOCKWISE, STARTING TOP RIGHT:
Anything handmade always has a place at the vintage
table. • The jeweled style of a cut pomegranate is a
natural addition to this sparkling vignette. • A warm
interior palette is dressed for the holiday with two
simply adorned trees. Both are live trees that will be
planted after the celebration.

feeling," says Audrey. "My thoughts are filled with past family get-togethers and the many memories gathered over the years. I try to create a mood, capture that feeling of warmth, love, and appreciation of nature and for family. Whether decorating a lush buffet table or a woodsy mantel scene, I work to create an overall feeling. It's actually quite spontaneous, as I look around my home, or at the McCharles House, and see the perfect item to work into a vignette—like a vintage necklace and brooch, a stack of old books, or a bejeweled bird figurine that normally rests on the bedroom dresser. I use natural items like pinecones, fresh-cut branches from the garden, and beautiful fruit and mix them with family treasures until I think I've captured the feeling I've been after."

Vivian Heredia, Audrey's daughter and the executive chef who makes flour into fantasy, also shares her mother's appreciation for the beauty found in vintage items. "I am captivated by the flicker of candlelight reflecting in jewel-toned glass beads. When guests arrive, I hope they swoon from the sugary scent of candy cane cookies still warm from the evening's baking," says Vivian. "I create an atmosphere with beautiful food displayed with Christmas ornaments amid family heirlooms; I want my guests to imagine Saint Nicholas brushing crumbs from white whiskers, a twinkle in his eye. I create a vignette where simple items are lifted to the magnificent, like the wonder of stockings spilling over with tangerines and candy and tin soldiers crafted by tiny elfin hands. It is my heart that

RIGHT AND OPPOSITE: Holiday style on the vintage table is a culmination of *warm* and *weathered* belongings lovingly collected and appreciated for their perfect imperfections.

PRECEDING PAGES: The sideboard is ready for a party with a combination of edibles and great pieces, notably a variety of footed cake plates, chunky candlesticks, and a vintage necklace decorating a tart plate.

helps me bring these magical visions to life as I hope to create memories for Christmases to come."

Timeworn pieces need not be the exclusive decorations on a vintage holiday table. Modern notes are found in a new imaginative spin such as silver feather trees and a vignette of glittered stars and paper cones made from old sheet music. At the Vintageweave Interiors, in Los Angeles, California, proprietress Kathy Delgado knows a few things about adding French flair to a table. "When it comes to a decorating style, my approach is always to do things in an unconventional manner," says Kathy. "Look for interesting antique and vintage Depression glass pieces and butter pats and then use them to hold votive candles. To unify the look, I'll stick with all clear glass but in different patterns. When treasure hunting, I seek out any clear vintage glass with a pedestal. A vintage wineglass, for instance, shouldn't be limited to its original use."

ABOVE AND RIGHT: For the
holidays, Carol Neiley uses simple
colors. Pine garlands are juxtaposed
with soft pink ranunculus to adorn the
mantle. Exotic fruits and nuts in simple
dishware on the table show brilliance in
a focus on special things. The entire
effect recalls Christmases past; even
Carol's dog takes in the dazzling
splendor.

OPPOSITE, BOTTOM: This
South American antique cupboard
contains the majority of Carol's pieces
that will have their play on the table.

Warm Settings

The holidays at Carol Neiley's home in Red Hook, New York, follow the two words in the name of her shop and online business: Basic French. This seeming oxymoron is telling in that there is a simple, easy, and elegant approach to the French lifestyle. "The simple French style is actually very spare," says Carol. "It's very minimalist, and they tend not to overclutter or to overstyle. Their look is more elegant as opposed to decorative."

When the holidays become a race against the clock—to buy and exchange with many festivities in between—a soothing environ-ment is the antidote to the chaos. "I work all the time. I am a single mother with two daughters and two dogs. I'm very casual about the things that I do. I'm monochro-matic and very simple about things."

Carol's ethic is deliciously applied to her table setting: white dishware, glasses, and the colors found in exotic fruits and flowers. She strays from brash reds and greens for a creamy palette that brightens the setting. A few traditions return every year, most nota-bly a trip to Exquisite Tarts in nearby Colum-bia County for her pastries and Battenfeld Christmas Tree Farm for princess pine.

Après-Ski

Rigorous outdoor activity of the winter variety always works up an appetite. Escape from the cold into a glamorous sanctuary with furs, feathers, and enough rich details that guests ask, "What deficit?"

Look to the Swiss Alps for inspiration, from its fine foods to its Alpine style. The table setting is the definition of easy luxury. With the precision of a fine timepiece, it looks great, works well, and won't let you down. Start with the table covering, which is a simple faux fur that will keep the animals calm. The tableware was selected to reflect the mountain environment through its classic, versatile design. After an active day, guests should be given the flexibility to be entertained yet feel relaxed. Thus, a spot by the fire may be more welcoming than a formal sit-down meal. Have a tray set up for easy movement.

Building on the winter's rich evergreens and brown color palette, add natural touches such as pinecones and pheasant and peacock feathers. This further enhances the rugged yet elegant Alpine-meets-Native-American theme. Read *The Last of the Mohicans* by James Fenimore Cooper for further inspiration.

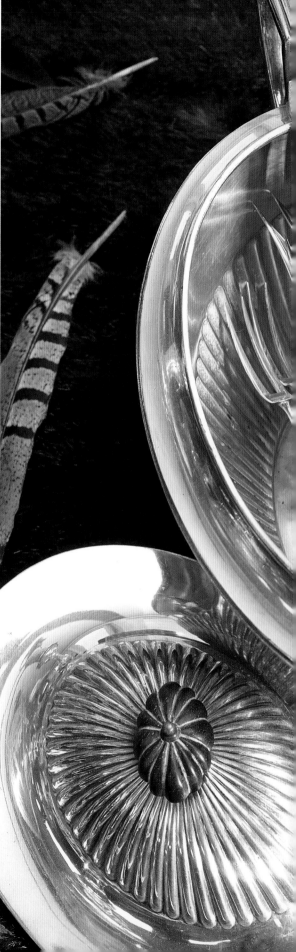

LEFT: Antique horn and silver cutlery from England are offered to guests in a soup tureen. ABOVE: A close look at the dishware divulges more of the *outdoors motif* carried throughout the party. BELOW: This authentic *Pomo treasure basket,* with bead and feather embellishments, adds a point of interest to the setting.

Get caught up in details. Store-bought roses combined with sprigs of pine, set in an elegant vase, have casual glamour. A silver soup tureen becomes the ideal vessel for antique horn-and-sterling cutlery. Throw in some decorative elements from around your home, such as mounted horns, a painting of a cabin, and anything with a stag theme, to add even more decorating drama.

Safe to say, no one will turn away a dish when its main ingredient is cheese. It can be served on a platter or in the warm and gooey melted style of fondue and raclette. Fondue parties are not just an opportunity to use a stowed-away registry item or a chance for men to wear turtleneck sweaters without looking like an illustration in a vodka ad. They also perform a valued function for this winter fete, since fondue is by nature a social activity. The fondue equipment can also be cleaned off and reused at the evening's close, for chocolate. Be sure to do all the prep work before-hand, especially cutting the bread and fruits for dipping.

Raclette is made by melting cheese and serving it with boiled new potatoes, cornichons, and onions. Making a raclette is an interactive and host-appreciated course, as guests are called upon to do the cooking without even realizing it. Using a raclette grill, the party congregates around the device, supervising their own meal until it is bubbling and ready. Raclette can also be made in a saucepan over an open fire, melting cheese the old-fashioned way. Place the cheese slices into oven-resistant metal pans (blini pans work well), and either heat them in an oven or place them close to the open flames of a fire. Add other foods such as mushrooms, onions, and peppers.

These diminutive *salt and pepper shakers* easily translate to a variety of settings.

"USING *unexpected* ITEMS, SUCH AS A BEER MUG FILLED WITH *feathers* AND FURS, WILL DISTINGUISH YOUR TABLE FROM THE RESERVATIONS-ONLY ESTABLISHMENT THAT REQUIRES YOU TO RISK ROADS FRESHLY KISSED BY *Jack Frost*."

An Entertaining Look Back

New Year's Eve is the perfect event for celebrating the vintage table, as it symbolizes a look back and a look at what's ahead—that classic blend of old and new. The holiday encapsulates all that this book has discussed, with its style, fun, and elegance. If there is one day of the year when you want to make time linger, New Year's Eve is it.

For an elegant New Year's Eve that is a modern take on mannered Victorian celebrations, fill your space with wintry details. Silver, gold, and the tones of a champagne bottle are an elegant and festive palette with a celebratory feel. Add complementary pieces such as polished candlesticks, sprigs saved from the Christmas tree, and holiday ornaments to build your vignettes. Also include symbolic details, such as old timepieces, a top hat, and the kind of walking stick Ebenezer Scrooge would have used.

Save the grocery store champagne and leave it to the kids in Times Square who blow whistles so tone challenged they'd scare off a goose. This gathering is as elegant and lovely as a ladies' ballroom glove. Here is a night when the strike of midnight signals the approach of new beginnings, a reason to keep the party going till sunrise, the most formidable way to cap the year.

Decadent nibbles should be available, such as figs and chocolates, all in tones that complement the setting. And as guests may still be there in the morning, fresh croissants and good strong coffee will also be appreciated.

↶ ABOVE LEFT: A bottle of *champagne* sets the tone of the evening.

↶ ABOVE RIGHT: Enameled *demitasse spoons* give vivid color to the otherwise natural palette.

↶ OPPOSITE, LEFT: New Year's Eve celebrations of a more elegant era looked much like this setting, complete with gleaming silver *candlesticks* and *lush evergreen* boughs. Oversized glass and mercury ornaments lend a playful feel to the vintage table.

↶ OPPOSITE, RIGHT: Trimming a New Year's table with decorative holiday *ornaments* is resourceful, elegant, and sparks memories of past celebrations.

TABLETOP DIARY WORKSHOP
THE SEASONS

This is the time to reflect, not only on all that you have composed in your diary but also on seasons past, present, and future.

Ideally, you have established your personal style, perfected your collection, and finessed your skills as a host. Now it's time to entertain regularly, and each season provides another cycle, an opportunity to be imaginative with the tabletop.

1. In your diary, DEVOTE AN ENTIRE SECTION TO EACH SEASON. Consider your favorite celebrations, and list these themes. These do not have to relate to an event connected to the tabletop. Every occurrence that builds a memory inspires.

2. Jot down your most MEMORABLE MOMENTS—the first Easter when you blew the yolks from eggs to create lifelong keepsakes, or a winter so cold you took cover indoors and perfected your Mother's recipes for pumpkin nut bread. If you have any scraps of personal memorabilia, such as photographs or handwritten recipes, put them into your diary.

3. Now consider this past year and the moments that INFLUENCED you. These can be as simple as a book you read or a concert you attended. Perhaps in that book there was a passage you found particularly poignant, which should be transcribed onto your page. The band may have performed a song that you can listen to ad infinitum; write down its lyrics. Now do you get it? These reflections have meaning. They create a happy feeling, and such moments can be shared with others.

An imaginative tabletop emerges from sharing something about yourself with your guests. Those words from a book can be handwritten, rolled up, and tied with twine, then left as a favor atop the dinner plates of your guests. Music can be played during the festivity. Your favorite song could be the new discovery appreciated by one of your guests, thereby perpetuating these small tokens of goodwill.

The seasons are more than periods that prompt you to make wardrobe adjustments. They renew the spirit and offer the chance for a fresh approach to your style and how you set the table.

CONCLUSION

*T*hough it may not be a spa nestled in the valley of a mountain range or a seacoast retreat, a stellar tabletop is like a serene sanctuary. On this tiny island, the world's axis seems to spin at a slower speed. Crystal and silver do dreamy things with light. Food tastes better when eaten from timeworn china. Added touches become loaded with implication, in the form of mint leaves punctuating a dessert plate, the metamorphosis of a napkin into a flower, or veggies cut into shapes that would get any child to eat his or her greens. The table's elements become the words composing a sonnet.

Conversation flows to the pleasant gush of wine. There will be talk about how pretty everything looks and how flavorful the soup is. The convivial chatter puts people at ease, so much so that intimacy sets in organically. A host is respected for her generosity and style. The dialogue turns to more substantive issues. New discoveries will be made about your dining companions, perhaps something that will have a profound influence on you.

A well-appointed table will bring people together, providing comfort and joy in their truest forms. This is a mannered place that has been in style since man first sought the company of others. Thought is put into the importance of ancestral hand-me-downs, and we acknowledge that the well-made is more valuable for its artistry than for its monetary worth. We suspend society's overwhelming preoccupation with consumption while attending a gathering that evokes awe. This is what can happen at a table with Vintage Vavoom.

Whether you are an avid entertainer or whether you just host the requisite holiday meals, this book will become an incentive to make this style of thoughtful, rich entertaining a custom in your home. Like a child who becomes a skilled writer from the enjoyment of reading, find a style that you love. You need not create it on a grand scale. The only requirement is that your tabletop reflects your personal flair.

RESOURCES

Shopping

ANN MARIE'S FINE
COFFEE AND TEA
Minocqua, Wisconsin
(800) 706,9993
www.annmarie.com

ANTHROPOLOGIE
Various locations
(800) 543,1039
www.anthropologie.com

ARTE ITALICA
Various locations
(212) 213,4773
www.arteitalica.com

BARBARA CHEATLEY'S
Claremont, California
(909) 621,4161

BASIC FRENCH
Red Hook, New York
(845) 758,0399
www.basicfrenchonline.com

THE BEAUTIFUL LIFE
Plant City, Florida
(888) 393,1133
www.thebeautifullife.com

BLISS LINENS
Corona del Mar, California
(949) 566,0380
www.blisslinens.com

BLUE CALICO
Online
(888) 825,7888
www.bluecalico.com

CAMPS AND COTTAGES
Carmel, California
(831) 622,0198
www.camps,cottages.com

CARY NOWELL
Ross, California
(415) 454,1402

COTTAGE WHITE
Sunset Beach, California
(562) 592,4678
www.cottagewhite.com

COUNTRY ROADS ANTIQUES
Orange, California
(714) 532,3041
www.countryroadsantiques
andgardens.com

DEAN & DELUCA
Various locations
(800) 221,7714
www.deandeluca.com

DEBRA'S COTTAGE
Costa Mesa, California
(714) 662,5828
www.debrascottage.com

DONALD KIRKBY
18TH C. ATELIER
Online
www.18thcatelier.com

EMBROIDERY PALACE INC.
West Hollywood, California
(310) 273,8003
www.embroiderypalace.com

FANTASY FLORAL DESIGNS
San Juan Capistrano, California
(949) 240,3571
www.fantasyfloraldesigns.com

FRENCH BLUE AND CO.
Online
www.frenchblueandco.com

THE FRENCH TULIP
San Francisco, California
(415) 647,8661
www.frenchtulip.com

GILDING THE LILY
Fullerton, California
(714) 680,8893
www.alainjamar.com/gildingthelily

HEAVENLY HOSTESS
Orange, California
(714) 538,8735
www.heavenlyhostess.com

HOME A LA MODE
Denison, Texas
(214) 542,5159
www.homealamode.com

HOUSE, INC.
Santa Monica, California
(310) 451,2597
www.houseinc.com

LADURÉE
Paris, France
www.laduree.fr

MATCH, INC.
Various locations
(201) 792,9444
www.match1995.com

MÉLANGE ANTIQUES
Laguna Beach, California
(949) 497,4915

MIDNIGHT SUN ANTIQUES
Libertyville, Illinois
(847) 362,5240
www.midnightsunantiques.com

NANCY KOLTES HOME
Various locations
www.nancykoltesathome.com

PANDORA DE BALTHAZAR
Pensacola, Florida
(850) 432,4777
www.antiqueeuropeanlinens.com

PARIS HOTEL BOUTIQUE
San Francisco, California
(415) 305,7846
www.parishotelboutique.com

P.O.S.H.
Chicago, Illinois
(312) 280,1602
www.poshchicago.com

QUEL OBJET
Briarcliff Manor, New York
(877) 762,4499
www.quelobjet.com

ROGER'S GARDENS
Corona del Mar, California
(800) 647,2356
www.rogersgardens.com

ROMANCE ETC.
Long Beach, California
(562) 439,5372
www.romance,etc.com

ROSANNA, INC.
Seattle, Washington
(877) 343,3779
www.rosannainc.com

ROSSI & ROVETTI FLOWERS
San Francisco, California
(415) 397,5311
www.rossirovetti.com

SADIE OLIVE
Online
(714) 730,7087
www.sadieolive.com

SENTIMENTAL CELEBRATIONS
Online
www.sentimentalcelebrations.com

SOMMER DESIGNS
Online
www.sommerdesigns.com

SOURCE PERRIER COLLECTION
Online
(888) 543,2804
www.sourceperrier.com

TROVE GALLERY
Laguna Beach, California
(949) 376,4640
www.trovelaguna.com

VIETRI
Various locations
(866) 327,1279
www.vietri.com

THE VINTAGE HOME
Online
(310) 376,5200
www.thevintagehomecollection.com

VINTAGEWEAVE INTERIORS,
INC.
Los Angeles, California
(323) 932,0451
www.vintageweave.com

VIVA TERRA
Online
(800) 233,6011
www.vivaterra.com

WHITNEY SMITH POTTERY
Various locations
(510) 208,2824
www.whitneysmithpottery.com

Restaurants

C'EST LA VIE RESTAURANT
Laguna Beach, California
(949) 497,5100
www.cestlavierestaurant.com

FORSTER MANSION
San Juan Capistrano, California
(949) 661,6676
www.forstermansion.com

GRACIE'S
Portland, Oregon
(503) 222,2171
www.graciesdining.com

THE McCHARLES HOUSE
Old Tustin, California
(714) 731,4063
www.mccharleshouse.com

THE RAMOS HOUSE
San Juan Capistrano, California
(949) 443,1342
www.ramoshouse.com

ACKNOWLEDGMENTS

Hillary Black and Jickie Torres, who walked beside me on the million steps it took to make this book come together without breathing a puff. To the one-of-a-kind talent found in the APG Media cadre, notably Elena Oh, Jaimee Itagaki, Merrie Destefano, and Meryl Schoenbaum. Amanda Heer is a genius with flowers. My editor, Aliza Fogelson, has that ability to make prose dance. Eleanor Jackson may be the closest I have to a fairy godmother, with her ability to grant wishes.

To the homeowners, proprietors, and style arbiters who allowed us into their homes and establishments, shared their special talents, and allowed us the liberty to make little adjustments for the sake of "the shot," my great appreciation.

And, of course, Allan Rosen, the man who graciously invited me into his home on my reconnaissance scout made via bicycle. Since that day, he and his daughter, Olivia, have allowed me to fuss and fudge, were withheld from eating pastries until after the shoot, and permitted me to move their beloved things with little controversy for the sake of a story. We now all live together happily, the best ending a book could have.

Photographers: Jaimee Itagaki, Ellen Silverman, Mark Tanner

Homeowners: Leif and Lynn Goldfinger-Abrams, Edward and Susan Beall, Laura Bowman, Adrienne and Ron Caldwell, Jeri Cunningham, Audrey and Vivian Heredia, Sue Jackson, Donald H. Kirkby, Kimberly Kotska, Bobby and Heather Lee, Lisa Mattice, Carol McEntire, Dennis and Nannette Myers, Carol Neiley, Kim Plant, Janet Rodriguez, Allan K. Rosen, Susan Schmidt, Janet and Larry Solomon, Annette Tatum, and Lucy and Tony Torres.

INDEX